T0099876

THE *Gift* OF SALVATION

Salvation A Gift from God

ANTONIO N. SHERMAN

WestBow
PRESS
A DIVISION OF THOMAS NELSON

Copyright © 2012 Antonio N. Sherman

All rights reserved. *No part of this book may be used or reproduced by any means, graphic, electronic, or mechanical, including photocopying, recording, taping or by any information storage retrieval system without the written permission of the publisher except in the case of brief quotations embodied in critical articles and reviews.*

WestBow Press books may be ordered through booksellers or by contacting:

WestBow Press
A Division of Thomas Nelson
1663 Liberty Drive
Bloomington, IN 47403
www.westbowpress.com
1-(866) 928-1240

Because of the dynamic nature of the Internet, any web addresses or links contained in this book may have changed since publication and may no longer be valid. The views expressed in this work are solely those of the author and do not necessarily reflect the views of the publisher, and the publisher hereby disclaims any responsibility for them.

Any people depicted in stock imagery provided by Thinkstock are models, and such images are being used for illustrative purposes only.

Certain stock imagery © Thinkstock.

ISBN: 978-1-4497-4769-5 (e)
ISBN: 978-1-4497-4770-1 (sc)
ISBN: 978-1-4497-4768-8 (hc)

Library of Congress Control Number: 2012906591

Printed in the United States of America

WestBow Press rev. date: 05/16/2012

Contents

A Testimonial from the Author

Why this book, *Salvation: A Gift from God*? Well, on the morning of December 21, 2009, being inspired in my spirit by the unction of the Holy Spirit, I felt the need to write it. Through my walk with God on my Christian journey to this present day, I have talked with many people who did not totally understand how and what takes place at salvation.

I have served God wherever he has led me, including in areas such as a Sunday school teacher, associate pastor, pastor, chief elder, usher, and minister. To me all that means and comes up to be one thing that I am proud of and privileged to be, and that's a *servant*. A lot of us miss that. And sadly to say, that include so-called church leaders of today. Being a servant of the Highest God, the True and Living God is something I do cherish, but truly am not worthy of, thanks be to God for sending His only begotten Son Jesus Christ that I am. I let it be known that I am a slave to Christ in a joyous state. But you may still ponder, *Why this book?*

Well, in explaining that, I want to share this experience with you: I was having a conversation with one of my fellow coworkers. He had just come in from the cold; literally, it was a very cold night. He shook my hand, and the conversation started. We talked about different books of wisdom; then the topic of religion came up. We talked about the Bible related to the movie industry.

He shared some of his beliefs with me. Now I felt the conversation beginning to change within. I felt something inside me started to churn. He said that he was of the Catholic faith. I just felt that there was something else going on in the spirit as we continued talking. So I said, "Okay. But what is your personal belief concerning the Bible?"

He said that he believes that there is a God, that Jesus is the Son of God, and that he believes in the Holy Spirit.

So I hesitated for a second, then I asked him, "Are you saved?" He started playing with his hand. He said, "I have never been saved; I have never been reborn." And I felt that unction in my spirit start rising up even more. But I also felt that he was confused and that he had a lack of understanding of what *salvation* was. I looked him straight in his eyes and said, "Today is your day."

Just as I was about to lead him to Christ according to Scripture, another of our coworkers suddenly entered the room. His countenance changed. I took his hand, still looking him in the eyes. I said, "Call me. You need to call me . . . anytime." He said, still holding on to my hand, "Yeah, I do . . . I will."

He knew who I was spiritually. We had worked together for over a year. He knew that I was a believer and a servant. And we have mutual respect for each other both on the job and off.

But doing our conversation that night, he allured to the fact that he truly understood neither salvation nor that God will forgive you for your sins. I remember telling him that it doesn't matter what sin you have committed. God will forgive you for it. You can't surprise him. All he wants you to do is come before him, confess it, turn away from it, and ask for his forgiveness.

He is surely faithful and just to forgive us for it. And during our conversation, I went on to say, "Don't let the enemy hold you there."

I could tell that he was lost in his understanding of the Word of God concerning this as well. He lacks the understanding of salvation as the gift from God.

On the morning of December 21, 2009, while I was receiving my daily bread from God, I felt the inspiration to write this book on *Salvation: A Gift from God*. I felt just like my coworker. There are many in such a state, not truly understanding salvation, even to the point of being confused about it.

So I pray that through the Holy Spirit of God, you, who are holding this book in hand right now, pray and ask God to open up your understanding of his gift of salvation, which was freely given to us all, and that from reading the chapters of *Salvation: A Gift from God*, you will be blessed, come to know Jesus Christ as personal Lord and Savior, and receive salvation as a gift from God.

And believing it by faith, giving Him the glory in Jesus name.

Amen

CHAPTER 1

NO OTHER NAME

We who are true believers know that the Holy Bible is the very breath of God. The Bible tells us in 2 Timothy 3:16-17 that "all scripture is given by the inspiration of God, and is profitable for doctrine, for reproof, for correction, for instruction in righteousness: That the man of God may be perfect, thoroughly furnished unto all good works."

So the infallible Word of God says, "Neither is there salvation in any other; for there is none other name under heaven given among men, whereby we must be saved" (Acts 4:12). Jesus said, "I am the way, the truth, and the life: no man cometh unto the Father, but by me" (John 14:6).

So what does that mean? What that means is this: There is no other way to the Father but by Jesus Christ, His only begotten Son. There is no other name given in all creation that one can use to receive salvation.

Plainly put, there is no other way to be saved but through Jesus Christ. There is no other way to the Father except through Jesus Christ, the Savior. Buddha is not the way; Allah is not the way; Muhammad is not the way; the pope is not the way. Neither can any of these names save you nor are they the way to the Father, God, who is in heaven.

The Scripture teaches that "for whosoever shall call upon the name of the Lord shall be saved" (Romans 10:13).

Not the name of your pastor, the bishop, the apostle, the minister, or the deacon! It's only the name of Jesus Christ.

Jesus is the way! I say to you to accept no other and nothing less. He is the truth and the life.

"For by grace are ye saved through faith; and that not of yourselves: it is the gift of God: Not of works, lest any man should boast" (Ephesians 2:8-9).

CHAPTER 2
WHAT IS SALVATION?

"Salvation (sal vâ/shen), n. salvatus, pp. of salvare, to save], 1. A saving or being saved; preservation from destruction; rescue. 2. a person or thing which is a means, cause, or source of preservation or rescue. 3. in theology, spiritual rescue from sin and death; saving of the soul through the atonement of Jesus; redemption."

Now, plainly put . . .

Salvation means wholeness, or rather, to be delivered and preserved from some type of destruction. There are no human beings on this earth who could save themselves or others from our present state of death and destruction or from the evil that surrounds us on a daily basis.

A person can be an exceptional "do-gooder," but no one can create a new heart or perfect nature that will save that individual from destruction. We can do nothing for ourselves; therefore, salvation is truly a gift from God. God's plan of salvation for the world can only be found in Jesus Christ, God's perfect sacrifice, the Lamb of God. He sent His Son as a living sacrifice to die on the cross in order to redeem humanity from the dominion of sin. He will save anyone who asks Him for that salvation.

3

Sin simply means that all of us are born with a fallen nature in that we all "miss the mark of perfection." We receive salvation by asking the Lord Jesus Christ to save us in an act of faith. This act of faith is a conviction that the gospel message of Christ is true, and we acknowledge our need for salvation and believe in our hearts that God sent His only begotten Son to save us.

A person is saved by grace, which is God's divine favor freely given to a person, no matter what that person has done in the past. The only way to forfeit salvation is to reject the gospel message of Jesus Christ.

Salvation is the gift of God to all who accept it through Jesus Christ, His Son!

CHAPTER 3
WHO NEEDS SALVATION?

The Word of God says that "all have sinned, and come short of the glory of God" (Romans 3:23). The Bible also tells, "Behold, I was shapen in iniquity; and in sin did my mother conceive me" (Psalm 51:5).

Why must we understand this?

The Bible teaches that "it is appointed unto men once to die" (Hebrews 9:27).

"The wages of sin is death; but the gift of God is eternal life through Jesus Christ our Lord" (Romans 6:23). There it is! Sin causes death.

Genesis 2:15-17 says, "And the Lord God took the man, and put him into the garden of Eden to dress it and to keep it. And the Lord God commanded the man, saying, Of every tree of the garden thou mayest freely eat: But of the tree of the knowledge of good and evil, thou shall not eat of it, for in the day that thou eatest thereof thou shalt surely die."

And let me say here that He meant a physical and spiritual death.

Now according to Romans 3:10-11, "as it is written, There is none righteous, no, not one: There is none that understandeth, there is none that seeketh after God."

You see, mankind is full of sinners by nature and by personal action, and none are righteous. Some may sin to a greater or lesser degree, but in God's eyes, sin is sin. And all have failed to attain to the standard of God, which is perfection of character, spiritual righteousness and performance. See Romans 3:9-23.

Romans also states that, "the wages of sin is death; but the gift of God is eternal life through Jesus" (6:23).

So who needs salvation? According to the Word of God, all of mankind does. Please allow me to expand more here in detail from the Bible.

All of mankind is condemned by God for sins committed and is subject to His divine judgment and wrath.

Romans 3:10: "As it is written, There is none righteous, no, not one."

Ephesians 2:3 says, "Among whom also we all had our conversation in times past in the lusts of our flesh, fulfilling the desires of the flesh and of the mind; and were by nature the children of wrath, even as others."

All of mankind is separated from God to the extent that they are not children of God, but of the devil.

John 8:44 says, "Ye are of your father the devil, and the lusts of your father ye will do. He was a murderer from the beginning, and abode not in the truth, because there is no truth in him. When he speaketh a lie, he speaketh of his own: for he is a liar, and the father of it."

All of mankind is captive and enslaved to the sin in our lives; we are not able to overcome the power of sin by our own efforts according to Romans 7: and John 8:31-36.

So what does all that mean? It means this: We need a Savior. There is nothing that we can do to save ourselves. Our works cannot save us. Therefore, we need to make a choice. And that choice is Jesus Christ. As it is stated within the Word of God in the book of Acts, there is no other name given under the heavens that one can be saved.

Our salvation comes through Him (Jesus). Not choosing is to already have chosen. The Bible teaches that we were born in sin. And it also teaches that the wages of sin is death. We know these truths form Scripture.

To procrastinate on accepting the Lord's salvation is dangerous! And it is the wrong choice, for no man knows the date or the hour that the Son of Man will return.

So who needs salvation? According to the written Word of God, we all do. And it's found in Jesus Christ.

He shed His blood for our redemption, our protection, our eternal life, and our salvation.

CHAPTER 4

WHO CAN HAVE SALVATION?

John 3:16 says, "For God so loved the world, that he gave his only begotten Son, that whosoever believeth in him should not perish, but have everlasting life." Please bear with me here a moment while I expand on this particular Scripture. I taught a Sunday school class on this Scripture one day at a church where I was invited by the pastor to come and minister.

This class related to the topic of salvation. After having the participants read John 3:16 out loud with me, I asked the question "What is the most important part of that Scripture?" I didn't ask if it was true, for we know that all of God's Word is true. The question was "What is the most important part of John 3:16?"

Some said that God was the most important part. I explained that God is always going to be God. He always was and is always going to be. Some said that "God so loved the world" was the most important, but I said no. His love doesn't change. He loves the world regardless. By reading the Scripture itself, you can see that being confirmed already. Someone also said, "Because he gave His only begotten Son." I still said no, because that decision was made before the beginning of time as we know it. To send Jesus into the world was not an afterthought of the Almighty God because man fell in the garden and handed over authority to the Devil. Sending Jesus into the world was a solution!

Now to answer the question, the answer is to believe. Everything else in the verse is a given. "God so loved the world [a biblical fact!] that he gave his only begotten Son" [another biblical fact!]. John 3:17 says, "For God sent not his Son into the world to condemn the world; but that the world through him might be saved." After Jesus was baptized in the Jordan River, God said, "This is my beloved Son, in whom I am well pleased." Now, let's finishing up John 3:16. "That whosoever believeth in him should not perish, but have everlasting life"—now this is something you must do! You must believe that He did; you must believe in Jesus to be saved. He can't believe for us. That part we must do ourselves. That's the most important part of John 3:16, to believe!

So who can have it? Who can have eternal life? Who can have salvation? The Scripture says, "whosoever believes." Please let us not miss that or confuse that. It's so simple that it takes a preacher to mess it up. He will save anyone who asks Him for that salvation.

Now, I want to lay before you one of the most important questions that has ever been asked to you up unto this day. And that is, are you one of those whosoevers? Are you one of those whosoevers who believe?

If so, praise God! But if not, please . . . please take a moment to read chapter 5 and say the prayer in chapter 12.

Jesus said that no man knows the date or the hour that the Son of Man will return: "But of that day and hour knoweth no man, no, not the angels of heaven, but my Father only" (Matthew 24:36). It could be before you turn the very next page! It could be before we take our very next breath.

The gift of salvation is for everyone who desires it. Let me show it to you biblically:

Romans 10:11-13: "For the scripture saith, Whosoever believeth on him shall not be ashamed. For there is no difference between the Jew and the Greek: for the same Lord over all is rich unto all that call upon him. For whosoever shall call upon the name of the Lord shall be saved."

You can see form those Scriptures alone that anyone can have the gift of salvation. Christ Jesus died for all.

The only way to forfeit salvation is to reject the gospel message (good news) of Jesus Christ.

Jesus paid the price for our salvation; He paid the price for our eternal freedom. In order for you to have everlasting life, there is nothing that you need to do except to receive the gift that He has already paid for. He died on the cross. God raised Him from the dead. And when you believe that, speak it, receive it, and confess Him publicly, you become "born again." You are now saved and are part of the family.

CHAPTER 5

HOW TO RECEIVE SALVATION

"No Formula, Just Biblical Facts"

First:

You must believe that Jesus Christ is the Son of God and that God raised Him from the dead. This is the basis of our Christian faith.

One thing to remember here is that Jesus was not created by God and sent to the earth as a man. Jesus has always existed with God and in actuality is a part of God.

John 1:1-3 says, "In the beginning was the Word, and the Word was with God, and the Word was God. The same was in the beginning with God. All things were made by him; and without him was not any thing made that was made."

Second:

You must repent of your sins. Repent means to turn away from your sins and stop doing them. Romans 6:23 says, "For the wages of sin is death; but the gift of God is eternal life through Jesus Christ our Lord." The payment for sin is death, but when you accept Jesus and repent of your sins, you receive eternal life. First John 1:9 says, "If we confess our sins, he is faithful and just to forgive us our sins, and to cleanse us from all unrighteousness." You must confess your sins and repent of them.

Third:

You must publicly acknowledge you have accepted Jesus Christ as your personal Savior. You see, being a Christian is not a hidden thing. It is not something that you do once and then deny the rest of your life. Becoming a Christian is a lifestyle. Romans 10:9 says, "If you confess with your mouth the Lord Jesus and believe in your heart that God has raised Him from the dead, you will be saved."

Please don't miss or overlook this very important part here.

It doesn't say "Believe in your heart and you will be saved." It says, "If you confess with your mouth . . . and believe in your heart that God has raised Him from the dead, you will be saved."

Jesus said, "Therefore whoever confesses Me before men, him I will also confess before My Father who is in heaven. But whoever denies Me before men, him I will also deny before My Father who is in heaven" (Matthew 10:32-33 NKJV).

We cannot hide our belief in Jesus Christ, in who He was when He walked the earth over two thousand years ago, and in who He is today.

Fourth:

By faith you must accept the gift of salvation that God has given to you. Ephesians 2:8 (NASB) says, "For by grace you have been saved through faith, and that not of yourselves; it is the gift of God." And John 1:12 (NASB) says, "But as many as received Him (Jesus), to them He gave the right to become children of God, even to those who believe in His name."

CHAPTER 6

YOUR ASSURANCE

What is our assurance of our salvation? To put it simple, God's Word is our assurance! His infallible Word. His unchanging Word. It's not a feeling. I have heard so many people whom I ministered to say this: "I don't feel saved." I am talking about those who say that they are Christian and have accepted Christ. And that is another reason for *Salvation: A Gift from God*—to help these people understand salvation and receive Jesus Christ as their personal Lord and Savior. Let me share the following experience with you to help you understand your assurance of your salvation. And let no one and nothing make you doubt your salvation.

"I recalled during my earlier walk with God. I was told by a bishop of a certain church. He knew I wasn't saved. I knew I was. I have been baptized according to Scripture. I've confessed all known sin and have accepted Jesus as my Lord and Savior. But yet being young and a babe in Christ, I was somewhat concerned about my salvation. I knew that I was saved. But to have had this bishop of this church that I was fellowshipping at to say this. I don't know why, but this made me start thinking. I was serving God as the sound technician and later on the choir.

So I started talking to God, flipping through the Bible and searching. I was frantic in wanting to know what made him make such a statement. I know I wasn't a habitual sinner.

And I recall to this day that as I was searching the Scriptures for certainty and assurance of my salvation, God spoke to my heart and spirit. He said, "My Word is your assurance." And when he said that, I felt at ease. I went back to the bishop and told him what God had said to me. I remember later hearing one of his messages making mention of that.

He said, "If you're waiting on me to tell you that you're saved, you are not. The burden of proof is on God." He has proved it. The proof is in His infallible Word.

"For whosoever shall call upon the name of the Lord shall be saved" (Romans 10:13).

CHAPTER 7

WITHOUT FAITH

Hebrews 11 is known as the faith chapter. Hebrews 11:6: "But without faith it is impossible to please him: for he that cometh to God must believe that he is, and that he is a re-warder of them that diligently seek him."

Ephesians 2:8: "For by grace are ye saved through faith; and that not of yourselves: it is the gift of God."

Scripture says that we are saved through faith. So without faith in what Jesus Christ did on the cross, it is impossible for one to be saved. Without faith in God's Word, it doesn't matter what else you believe concerning salvation—it amounts to nothing. Why? Well, first of all, we must have faith in order to please God. God is moved by faith. But we must remember, as taught in the book of James, that faith without works is dead. Not that your works can saved you. You see, *faith* is an action word, just like *love*. It must be shown. It must be put to work. It's something that must be done. Without faith we cannot receive the gifts and blessing of God.

And it's not that He hasn't already given them. It's that we haven't done our part of believing by faith and receiving them. Simply put, we must have faith to receive from God. Throughout the Bible, faith is talked about from Genesis to Revelation. Our faith is very important pertaining to our receiving the gift of salvation.

What were Jesus' remarks to Peter once He reached out and saved him from sinking after stepping out on the water? Once back in the boat, Jesus asked where his faith was and why he doubted.

When Jesus was asleep in the boat with his disciples, the storm began to rage and they became afraid and cried, "Lord! Lord! You care not we perished?" Jesus stood up, stretched out his arms, and spoke to the winds, "Peace, be still." He stated, "Ye of little faith."

There are numerous counts where the question of faith is mentioned and taught by our Lord Jesus. So I encourage you to please read what is known as the faith chapter, Hebrews 11, and study the Word of God on faith. But do come to know that "without faith it is impossible to please God" (Hebrews 11:6 NIV).

CHAPTER 8

BELIEVE OR NOT!

Believing is so important that it is mentioned throughout the Bible. It is also one of the key factors to why today churches do not see much of the miracles that took place in the early church days.

Not believing is such a main part of this that the Bible stated that even Jesus himself could only do but a few miracles in his home town (Matthew 13:58).

Hebrews states that those who come to God must believe that he is. (Hebrews 11:6).

I thought that this topic is so important that I put this chapter in this book concerning salvation. I want to expand on the fact that just because we choose not to believe on a thing or in a thing, we do not exactly stop it from being. When it comes to Bible facts, whether we choose to believe them or not, they will still come to pass or they still do exist.

If one chooses not to believe in God, it doesn't change the fact that He is and always will be. In the same way, if one states that one doesn't believe that Jesus Christ is not the Son of God, it does not change the eternal biblical fact that He surely is.

Now in relating this to salvation, it is not about believing only but about receiving as well. Salvation is a gift from God through Jesus

Christ, His Son, for all who believe and receive it by faith. The work for our salvation is done by Jesus. Whether we choose to believe it or not will not change those biblical facts. But whether one chooses to believe it or receive it will sure enough make an eternal decision as to where one will spend eternity.

And that fact will not be changed by whether one believes or not.

We must understand that everlasting life doesn't just mean living forever. You will live forever anyway, whether you believe in Jesus or not. The question is where you will live. Will you live forever in His presence, in the glory of heaven, or will you live for all eternity separated from Him and His love? One way is eternal life. The other is eternal death. Please let's don't miss these facts. And let no man deceive you with vain words or false hope. Your only hope is in Jesus Christ.

CHAPTER 9

THE GIFT

The Holy Bible speaks of different gifts from Genesis to Revelation. Please take notice of the following Scriptures:

1 Corinthians 12 talks about different spiritual gifts. 1 Corinthians 12:1: "Now concerning spiritual gifts, brethren, I would not have you ignorant." It's mentioned throughout the whole chapter how different gifts are given by the one same Spirit. The book of Acts talks about the gift of the Holy Spirit.

In Acts 10:45, the circumcised believers who had come with Peter were astonished that the gift of the Holy Spirit had been poured out even on the Gentiles.

In Acts 2:38, Peter replied, "Repent and be baptized, every one of you . . . And you will receive the gift of the Holy Spirit" (NIV).

1 Corinthians 12:9: "To another faith by the same Spirit, to another . . ." (NIV). "The same Spirit gives great faith to another, and to someone else the one Spirit gives the gift of healing" (NLT).

Ephesians 3:16: "I pray that out of his glorious riches he may . . ." (NIV). "I'm asking God to give you a gift from the wealth of his glory. I pray that he would give you inner strength and power through his Spirit" (GW).

1 Corinthians 12:11: "All these are the work of one and the same . . ." (NIV). "It is the one and only Spirit who distributes all these gifts. He alone decides which gift each person should have" (NLT).

So as you can see from reading the Scriptures above, the Bible talks about receiving gifts from God. But the gift that I am referring to in this book and chapter is the gift of salvation.

Please read the following Scriptures and get a clear biblical understanding of this issue. And know that salvation is something that you cannot obtain by works per se. I've been a good person all my life. I give to the needy. I pray all the time. I read the Bible every day and sing on the choir. And I never said a bad word in my whole life! But to top it all off, I led one thousand souls to Christ! So I earned my gift, right? No, wrong!

Good deeds and great work—yes. But please read the following Scripture and see how you're saved and how to receive the gift of salvation.

Ephesians 2:8-9: "For by grace are ye saved through faith; *and that not of yourselves*: it is the gift of God: *Not of works*, lest any man should boast".

Romans 3:24: "And are justified freely by his grace through the . . ." (NIV). "Being justified as a gift by His grace through the redemption which is in Christ Jesus . . ." (NASB). "Put to their credit, freely, by his grace, through the salvation which is . . ." (BBE).

Yet often Christians, even after they have been given the gift of salvation, feel obligated to try to work their way to God. We must understand that our salvation and even our faith are gifts. And we should respond with love, joy, gratitude, praise, and worship.

Our salvation is a gift from God, and a gift is something that is freely given. If it has a condition attached to it, then it is no longer free.

Telling others about Christ and remembering or knowing your exact date of salvation are not conditions of salvation but should be the result of salvation as we grow in his grace.

A good book to read on this is *21 Things God Never Said: Correcting Our Misconceptions about Evangelism* by R. Larry Moyer. You have a gift only if there are no strings attached to it.

CHAPTER 10

THE SEAL, THE PROMISE, AND YOUR GUARANTEE

When we were first born again, we received the Holy Spirit into our spirits. This is known as the salvation measure of the Holy Spirit that every believer receives. When Peter preached his first sermon, he said to the people, "Repent, and let every one of you be baptized in the name of Jesus Christ for the remission of sins; and you shall receive the gift of the Holy Spirit." The gift of the Holy Spirit is given at the point when we received Jesus.

2 Corinthians teaches us that God gives us His Spirit and seals us with His Spirit as a guarantee that we belong to Him.

Let's read it from the King James Version of the Holy Bible texts.

2 Corinthians 1:22: "Who hath also *sealed* us, and given the earnest of the Spirit in our hearts".

The phrase "the earnest" means *as a deposit*. Now let's see what it says in Ephesians pertaining to the seal and promise concerning our salvation.

Ephesians 1:13: "In whom ye also trusted, after that ye heard the word of truth, the gospel of your salvation: in whom also after that ye, *believed*, ye were *sealed* with that holy Spirit of promise" (my italics).

You have the written Word of God. But God also gives us a deposit, and that is His Holy Spirit.

In Acts the question was, what shall we do? "Now when they heard this, they were pricked in their heart, and said unto Peter and to the rest of the apostles, Men and brethren, what shall we do? Then Peter said unto them, Repent, and be baptized every one of you in the name of Jesus Christ for the remission of sins, and ye shall receive the gift of the Holy Ghost" (Acts 2:37-38).

Which is your assurance, your deposit?

"For the promise is unto you, and to your children, and to all that are afar off, even as many as the Lord our God shall call" (Acts 2:39).

The Holy Bible teaches us that it is impossible for God to lie. (Titus 1:2 and Hebrews 6:18)

Why is this fact so important? Well, by knowing and believing that it is impossible for Him to lie, you know that your salvation is secure through Christ Jesus. Two Timothy 3:16: "All scripture is given by the inspiration of God, and is profitable for doctrine, for reproof, for correction, for instruction in righteousness: That the man of God may be perfect, thoroughly furnished unto all good works."

And to all who were lead to pick up this book, I want to say and share this with you: Know that your salvation is given as a gift from a True and Living God who is omnipresent, omnipotent, and omniscient. As I was meditating on all of this, this word was dropped in my spirit: "omniperfect" (God is all-perfect). How can you not call on Him and accept this gift through Jesus Christ?

"And do not grieve the Holy Spirit of God, by whom you were sealed for the day of redemption" (Ephesians 4:30 ESV).

CHAPTER 11

A PRAYER FOR SALVATION

To accept Jesus as your personal Lord and Savior,
pray this prayer from your heart.

Lord Jesus, you said in your Word that those who come to you, you will no way turn back on. And you said that whosoever calls upon your name shall be saved.

Lord, I come to you, and I am calling upon your name right now, asking that you please forgive me for my sins. I repent, turning away from them. I believe that you are the Son of the True and Living God, died for my sins, and were raised on the third day.

Jesus, I invite you into my heart to be my Lord and Savior. And I am asking that you save me and fill me with the Holy Spirit.

I turn from my sins and now live for you.

For you said that if I confess with my mouth that you are Lord and believe this in my heart, I shall be saved.

I thank you for saving me, taking me out of the kingdom of darkness and placing me into the kingdom of light. According to your Word, I am now a new creature, and old things are passed away.

I receive this gift of salvation by faith. In Jesus' name. Amen.

CHAPTER 12

A WORD OF ASSURANCE
AND ENCOURAGEMENT

Whoever you are and wherever you may be, no matter what you may have done, if you have just said this prayer from your heart and meant it, know that you are now saved.

It's not about a feeling but about believing and receiving what Jesus Christ did on the cross over two thousand years ago for us all. If you believe that and receive it, salvation is yours.

My advice now to you is that you find yourself a good Bible-teaching ministry and continue your personal walk and growth in God. Join a good Bible study group, attend Sunday school, and have continuous one-on-one prayer and fellowship with the Father.

Visit us at www.yourdailybread4life.com for a daily bread of encouragement. And join our weekly live Ustream.tv ministry broadcast, *Our Daily Bread*. If you don't have anyone with whom you can share the good news that you have accepted Jesus Christ as your personal Lord and Savior. Please write to us at: I want to rejoice with you just as the angels in heaven do each time another is reborn. And I want to give you a personal letter from Him to you.

CHAPTER 13

ONE STEP FARTHER (NEVER AGAIN)

The last part of *Salvation: A Gift from God* is titled "God's Words of Encouragement." I decided to start it off with a few pages of a section I entitled "My Never Agains." Now that you understand salvation and have received it through believing in and accepting Jesus Christ as your personal Lord and Savior, there are some never agains I want to share with you.

But before we get into this teaching that I have prepared for you, I want to share some biblical facts with you, some of which you may already know and some you may not. In doing so, we must come to the understanding that God's Word will not change. He has promised that they will not return to Him void. They will accomplish that which it was sent to do. We also must understand that God's Word will not change, whether we choose to believe in them or not.

This goes for the saved and the unsaved, saint or not. God is always going to be God. He always was and always will be; He is the Alpha and Omega. The Bible teaches us that heaven and earth will pass away before one letter of His Word changes.

So what does all that has to do with this section of the book? Well, the Bible teaches us that life and death are in the power of the tongue, in the words that we speak or say. Words are spirits, and with them, we either bring blessings or curse. And guess what. Believe it or not, the words that you and I speak or say will either bring life or death, blessings or curse. The Word of God teaches you this. And it is something that is gravely overlooked or taken lightly.

We who walk by faith and not by sight must understand that the confessions of our mouth will eventually bring forth the fruit of our lips. So where am I taking you with all this? The point is to lead you into a deeper understanding of what is known as "Bible confession" and into "God's Words of Encouragement" inside this book of salvation.

I want to lead you into agreement with what the Word of God has said about you. So *Believe In the Promises of God and Walk In Them* (another Spirit book I was blessed to write). "And was charged to go tell my people," says the Lord.

So Never Again

Never again will I confess "I can't," for "I can do all things through Christ which strengtheneth me."
Philippians 4:13

Never again will I confess lack, for "my God shall supply all [my] need according to his riches in glory by Christ Jesus."
Philippians 4:19

Never again will I confess fear, "for God hath not given us the spirit of fear; but of power, and of love, and of a sound mind."
2 Timothy 1:7

Never again will I confess doubt and lack of faith, for "God hath dealt to every man [person] the measure of faith."
Romans 12:3

Never again will I confess weakness, for "the Lord
is the strength of my life."
Psalm 27:1

"The people that know their God shall be strong, and do exploits."
Daniel 11:32

Never again will I confess lack of wisdom, for "Christ Jesus,
who of God is made unto us wisdom . . ."
1 Corinthians 1:30

Never again will I confess supremacy of Satan over my life,
for "greater is he that is in [me], than he that is in the world."
1 John 4:4

Never again will I confess defeat, for "God . . .
always causeth [me] to triumph in Christ."
2 Corinthians 2:14

Never again will I confess sickness,
for "with his stripes [I am] healed."
Isaiah 53:5

Jesus "Himself took [my] infirmities, and bare [my] sicknesses."
Matthew 8:17

Never again will I confess worries and frustrations.
I am "casting all [my] care upon him; for he careth for [me]."
1 Peter 5:7

Never again will I confess bondage, for "where the
Spirit of the Lord is, there is liberty."
2 Corinthians 3:17

Never again will I confess condemnation, for "there is therefore
now no condemnation to them which are in Christ Jesus."
Romans 8:1

Never again will I confess loneliness. Jesus said, "Lo, I am with you always, even unto the end of the world."
Matthew 28:20

"I will never leave thee, nor forsake thee."
Hebrews 13:5

Never again will I confess curses or bad luck, for "Christ hath redeemed us from the curse of the law, being made a curse for us . . . That the blessing of Abraham might come on the Gentiles through Jesus Christ; that we might receive the promise of the Spirit through faith."
Galatians 3:13-14

Never again will I confess discontent, because "I have learned, in whatsoever state (circumstances) I am, therewith to be content."
Philippians 4:11

Never again will I confess unworthiness, because "He hath made him to be sin for us, who knew no sin; that we might be made the righteousness of God in him."
2 Corinthians 5:21

In knowing all this, remember that faith comes by hearing the Word of God. So let us study to show yourself approved before God, a workmen made, not a shame. In confessing God's Word, you're confessing Him for He is His Word. So stand on the Rock (Jesus) and be not moved, being rooted and grounded in the faith. And never again forget who you are in Christ Jesus, giving God glory!

CHAPTER 14

GOD'S WORDS OF ENCOURAGEMENT

Be Encouraged . . . All Is Well!

When you feel alone, dealing with low self-esteem, or just think that no one cares, know that you are precious in God's eyesight. Just turn to the Word of God in these times of need. I am here to tell you that you are priceless to Him and that He loves you unconditionally. The Word of God tells us that nothing in all creation can separate us from His love. Romans 8:38-39: "I am convinced that neither death nor life, neither angels nor demons, neither the present nor the future, nor any powers, neither height nor depth, nor anything else in all creation, will be able to separate us from the love of God that is in Christ Jesus our Lord" (NIV).

Young people, the Word of God tells you not to let anyone despise (look down on) you because of your youth, but to set an example in speech, meaning in the things you say and how you say them. Sadly nowadays it is a fact that young people will say anything to anybody, to parents and others in authority, even to the Lord.

But I appeal to you, my sons and daughters, instead be that positive influence that others around would want to emulate.

I remember sitting in the company of two young females on a visit to Orangeburg, South Carolina, with my wife. The topic of music came up, and one of the females stated how she loved this hot new song by a well-known artist that had just come out. The younger of the two females responded with, "Oh, I don't listen to that kind of music anymore." As I watched the expression on the face of the slight older female who just know that the younger was into what she was. But instead she chooses to be the example of a young Christian female in spike of her age.

This brings me to the point of saying this: In spite of your youth, be an example in faith, believing God's Word and what He says about you in it and holding on to it, no matter what. Yes, that means holding out against peer pressure from friends and family members. I pray for all to hold on to our faith. Why? Simply because the Bible teaches us that he who endures to the end is saved. It states that the first shall be last and the last shall be first.

We know that many are called but only a few are chosen. It doesn't matter what life look like now. Just keep believing, praying, fasting, and reading God's Word, the Holy Bible. And lastly on this topic, young people, be an example in purity. Be pure in heart and mind. Let nothing enter in that would cause you to live otherwise to what has just been said. Renew your mind with His Word and conform not to the image (likeness) of this world, but be transformed from it. "This is what the Lord says—he who created you . . . he who formed you . . . I have redeemed you; I have summoned you by name; you are mine . . . you are precious and honored in my sight and . . . I love you" (Isaiah 43:1-4). I want you to know that our life has purpose. The Word of God says that we are His workmanship created in Christ Jesus to do good works, which God has prepared in advance for us to do. This can be found in (Ephesians 2:10).

So no matter where you may be in life and what you may have done in life, no matter what you may have been taught. I'm saying "taught" because some of us have been taught some erroneous principles concerning the Word of God. And to those who have done so and are still doing so, I will give an account thereof.

But above all, I want you to mediate on this: "You, O Lord created my innermost being, you knit me together in my mother's womb. I praise you because I am perfect fully and wonderfully made." And to those of you who were led to be holding this book in your hands this very minute, please read Psalm 139:14-14.

Yes, I do know and understand that life can be hard at times. Please believe me when I say this. I have experienced it as many of you have. But faith in Him (Jesus Christ) and the written Word of God can cause you to rise above the occasion no matter what it is.

Some of you may be thinking right now, *But he just don't know!* Maybe I don't, but He does. I want to assure you that there is not anything that takes place in all creation that God is not aware of. He is an all-knowing God. He is omnipresent, which means that He is everywhere all at once. He is omnipotent, which means that He is all-powerful. He is omniscient, which means that He has all knowledge. And while I was meditating on His Word during one of my daily studies, it was placed within my spirit that God is not just perfect but all-perfect—He is "omniperfect"!

And I want you to know that God does have Satan in check. If you want to read more on this truth, read Job and ask God to reveal to you the meaning of Satan's appearance before God asking permission to come up against Job.

Having said that, once again I want to let you know that, yes, life can be hard at times. It may seem that no one cares that you're hurting. But I want to employ you to consider the Word of God before you consider doing anything else that may cause harm to yourself. I am talking both physically and spiritually. Consider what the Word of God says about you before turning to any kind of substance abuse or anything else as a means of escape. I want you to know that drugs, alcohol, sexual activities, or anything else cannot bring that to you.

If you would, please allow me a few minutes to minister here. I feel it is very important to shed some light on sex and self-esteem. I must go there because there are so many women, young and old alike, who feel giving themselves up sexually would make them feel wanted or needed, even loved. The Devil is a liar! You don't have to go there! Let me tell you, my sisters who feel this way or even think continuingly this way: Please don't!

I feel the need to say that if that person really cares for you and loves you as he is expressing, then it shouldn't have to take your giving yourself sexually to prove it. I must put it this way, for nowadays young women are flipping the coin in the persistence concerning this as well. Is that shocking? Well, if so, what I am about to say next will shock you even more. You must agree with me about what I just said about low self-esteem and sex. It's all around us. We can see it everywhere—in our schools, on the job, and in church! No, that wasn't the shocker! The apostle Paul addresses this issue to the church of Corinth. The shocker is that yet in this present day and age, there are men out there who will prey on this type of women, whether save or unsaved. And a lot of it takes place right in the household of faith, the church. It's a known fact but sad that everyone who walks through the doors of the church does not come to seek Jesus the Christ or to praise and worship God the Father. Let the truth be told, some women come to church because they have heard that plenty of good-looking men are attending there. Some men go because they hear that there're a lot of women attending. I am speaking across the board, but I am dealing with men in this particular text. Yes, there're certain women walking here as well. But there are many so-called men of God who will take advantage of women who are living in this state who are seeking to rise above this issue wanting help.

Please don't close the book now. Let the truth be told. It is the truth that will set you free. Deliverance is on the way! Women, my sisters, you don't have to stay there. Meditate on this: "O Lord, when I consider your heavens the work of your fingers, the moon and the stars which you have set in place, what is man that you are so mindful of him, the Son of Man whom you care for? Lord, you made him little lower than the heavenly beings and crowned him with your glory and honor. You made him ruler over the work of your hands; you put everything under his feet—all flock and herbs, the birds of the field and the air, the fish of the sea, and all that swims the path of the sea."

Now I want you to just think about that and know that you are special and loved dearly in His eyesight.

If that's not enough to lift your low self-esteem, then know that you are valuable enough to God that He gave the life of His only Son. Those of you who are parents, let me ask you just one serious question: Can you give the life of your child for someone else? Even for some that you already know will not believe in Him. Can you give up your child to be punished for something that he or she didn't do? Just to show them that you love them. To show that their live have meaning and value to Him. Ponder that for just a minute.

Salvation . . . !

Know that the Creator of the universe paid the highest price that can be paid to give you the choice to experience a personal relationship with Him through Jesus Christ. So lift your head up—you're priceless. He knows all about you, the good and the bad, but yet paid the price because He loves you!

In Isaiah 35:4, the Word of God says to those who are fearful heart, "Be strong, fear not: behold, your God will come with vengeance, even God with a recompence; he will come and save you."

The Lord wants you to know that "ye are a chosen generation, a royal priesthood, an holy nation, a peculiar people; that ye should shew forth the praises of him who hath called you out of darkness into his marvellous light" (1 Peter 2:9).

He also wants you to be "confident of this very thing, that he which hath begun a good work in you will perform it until the day of Jesus Christ" (Philippians 1:6). I know it may seem easy to turn to other sources to try and lift you up, or get you to feel important. Please know that these things are only temporary fixes if any at all, if I may use that term here. But a permanent solution can only come from the Word of God. Why can I make that statement? Well, within the Word of God is found the answer to every issue of life. We must learn to turn to the Word of God in time of need, whether it's for guidance, counseling, direction, healing, deliverance, or encouragement. He wants you to hold on to your confidence. Hebrews 10:35 says, "Cast not away therefore your confidence, which hath great recompence of reward." So study the Word of God and believe what it says about you. Be encouraged of your worth in life, for you have been predestined. To put it plainly, you were thought of and destined to a purpose in life for God, even before birth. Please don't miss this fact!

Jeremiah 29:11 says, "For I know the thoughts that I think toward you . . . thoughts of peace, and not of evil, to give you an expected end." The Bible says what matter of love that he has bestowed upon. That even the angels wanted to know this. Let me take you to the Word of God and let Him answer a question that may be pressing on your mind. No matter where you are, I want you to stop and think on this, but not only that. I want you to see for yourself the answer to the question of how great His love is for you. So please stop right now, find a Bible, turn to Psalm 103, and see the magnitude of his love for you.

Oh my God! I love Him! I know where He has brought me from and where I should have been! God is truly good! It's so great that I cannot even totally express it. All I can say is that for all that He has done and is still doing in our lives, even when we don't see or feel it, He's there, and it is overwhelms me.

I must say from firsthand experience, if He has ever touched your live, His love—not your love or our love, but His love—just compels you to want do what is right and pleasing to Him. In my earlier years with Christ—just grasping true understanding of His love for me and for us all—I truly understood what John meant when he said in Revelation that "he became undone." Just in the presence of God, I truly felt the love of God and was unable comprehend it to the point that all I knew was that it was like nothing I had ever felt. His love shows us that what we call love is not truly love. Holy Father, teach us your agape love!

His loves draws you toward Him. I was lost in sin and blind, and really couldn't see. And yet, even then He kept telling me through His Word, "You're precious to me, and priceless. I love you." I thank Jesus Christ for being obedient, even to death on the cross! Even then He (God) sent back His sweet Holy Spirit to continue to comfort us, to help us, and to lead us. He said, "I will not leave you comfortless. I will come to you. I am here. Be still; have faith. Be still and know that I am God."

Even though your friends and family may sometimes leave you or forsake you when push comes to shove, I want to share with you some encouraging words on this. Please take some time to read and study the following Scriptures. These are from John 14 and this is our Lord Jesus talking. "I will send you another comfortable." He says he will never leave you. (John 14:16) The world at large can't recognize Him. (John 14:17) He teaches us. (John 14:26) He glorifies Jesus. (John 16:14)

After the day of Pentecost (Acts 2), He came to live in all believers. Please take a little time for Jesus and read the whole chapter of John 14. Jesus prays and tells of many promises that have taken place and will take place. Many people, including believers, are unaware of the activities of the precious Holy Spirit of God on earth and in our lives. I want you to come to know these activities according to the written Word of God. From the Word of God, know that to those who receive Christ and come to understand the Spirit's power in their Christian life, He gives a whole new way to look at life as a

Christian life as a true follower of Jesus Christ. Hallelujah! "He will abide with you forever."

The Holy Bible is a great reservoir of the power of God; every time you feed your spirit on the Word of God, it grows stronger. Think why our Lord and Savior Jesus said during His temptation by the Devil, "It is written, Man shall not live by bread alone, but by every word that proceedeth out of the mouth of God" (Matthew 4:4).

Physical bread feeds your natural body. The Word of God is food for your soul. Your spirit needs to be feed just as your natural body. You see, it is the spirit that is quicken (made alive) the flesh profit little according to the Word of God. Jesus said, "The words that I speak unto you, they are spirit, and they are life" (John 6:63).

Please allow me to do a little teaching as the Spirit leads. I want you to know that victory over the world, over the flesh, and over the Devil comes through the Word. And know that Jesus is the living Word. The Word of God is the most tangible and powerful weapon that God has given us. It's the sword of the Spirit. The enemy cannot penetrate the Word of God when it is spoken in faith. When we confess what the Word says, when we speak what the Word says, and when we come in agreement of what the Word of God says, we unlock the door of faith, putting God's Word in to action. You see, faith must be release to work. Faith is an action word. This brings me to the point of that we should always speak well to ourselves about ourselves. Never speak words of doubt. Why? Remember that the Word of God teaches us that "life and death are in the power of the tongue." Many of us forget that fact often. We throw our words around loosely, not knowing the path we're laying for ourselves.

The Bible tells us not only that "life and death are in the power of the tongue" but also that for every idle word we speak, we will give an account on the day of judgment. Our words are important. Jesus said, "I only speak what the Father says. The words that I speak are not my own."

I have met and talked with all kinds of people, both saved and unsaved. They don't even realize that they are bringing death and destruction upon themselves by their own words. By the words of their mouth, "this thing is going to kill me yet," "I am going to die from this thing," "that is going to be the death of me," "I am never going to do this or get this done."

So, so innocent? But guest what eventually it all comes true. Sounds harsh? Sometimes reality is. Get to the reality of God's Word. "Life and death are in the power of the tongue: and they that love it shall eat the fruit thereof" (Proverb 18:21). We must believe that there is power in the Word of God.

From the Bible we know that with a word, God spoke the world in to existence as we know it.

He said, "Let there be," and it was. He placed high value on His Word. He also said to me doing my earlier walk with him. "He said I watch over my word to see that it comes to pass." He teaches us in His written Word that "you are who I said that you are in Christ and have what I said that you have in Him." Another biblical fact that I want to interject is that we are all God's creation, whether saved or unsaved. Saved, having accepted and received Christ Jesus as your personal Lord and Savior, the enemy has no right to you. Unsaved, not having accepted Jesus as your personal Lord and Savior, you'll become a play tool for the enemy. I'm not saying that he doesn't attempt to come up against us once we become Christians. But know that you are sealed and protected divinely under the wings of the Almighty, as so stated in Psalm 91. Please take some time and meditate it.

Remember that the Word of God tells us that we are created in His image, in His likeness. God is the Creator. Know this as well to ensure you pertaining to His Word: "For the word of God is quick, and powerful, and sharper than any twoedged sword, piecing even to the dividing asunder of soul and spirit, and of joints and marrow, and is discerner of the thoughts and intents of the hearts" (Hebrews 4:12).

So what does all of this mean? Simply put, it means that the Word of God is not just a collection of words from God, or a means of communicating ideas to us. But it is life-changing! And it's dynamic, as it works in us with the incisiveness of a surgeon's knife! The Word of God reveals who we are and what we are not! I wrote this book through the inspiration of the Holy Spirit because of the ministry that was born within my heart by the Holy Spirit years ago. That was and still is the Ministry of Helps and Encouragement. If it had not been so, and if I had thought differently, trust me, I would have not done so. I would have not have wasted the paper.

I wrote this book solely to encourage, edify, and build up others. God sent His Word to instruct us, to lead us, and to be a guide and lamp for our feet. "Thy word is a lamp unto my feet, and a light unto my path" (Psalm 119:105).

Yes, even from the beginning of time as we know it, there has been a consequence for not being obedient to the Word of God. But there is repentance and forgiveness for all who really want and desire it.

Now let me share something personal with you. On January 21, 2005, two years from the date God told me to "go tell my people to believe in Me, in My Word, in My promises. And just walk in them, for I have already given them to you." It was on the night of January 21, 2003, that He laid heavily on my heart what one of my gifts of the Spirit to the body of Christ was.

The apostle Paul taught on this in 1 Corinthians 12:28: "And God hath set some in the church, first apostles, secondarily prophets, thirdly teachers, after that miracles, then gifts of healings, helps, governments, diversities of tongues." The Spirit works through us through different gifts for the body as we yield ourselves to Him. And He revealed to me that mine was that of helps and encouragement.

The morning of January 22, 2003, He confirmed it through His Word. He took me to that particular chapter. He made me to understand through studies that all gifts were given for the perfecting of the saints and the working of the ministry. In 1 Corinthians 12:31, apostle Paul made it clear that one gift is not superior to another. God has given them by the Holy Spirit. Your spiritual gift is not for your own personal self-advancement, but is given to you for serving God and enhancing the spiritual growth of the body of believers. Above all, I have come to know that the gift is holy, for it is of God.

Sadly we don't see most of the gifts working because of unbelief of the believers. A missionary, a minister of God, once gave a testimony of how the power of God had been working and moving while he was out in the field and how he had seen the sick healed, the lame walk, sight restored, and even the dead brought back to live! Another of the men listening to the missionary's account spoke up and said, "Now that's hard to believe." The missionary calmly turned to face him and said, "And that is why you haven't seen such mighty acts of God." This is a true account of an event that took place.

Lastly, I must add the following concerning the gifts of the Spirit: First Corinthians 13:1 says, "Love is more important than all the spiritual gifts exercised in the church body. Great faith, acts of dedication or sacrifice, and miracle-working power have little effect without love. Love makes our actions and gifts useful. Although people have different gifts, love is available to everyone" (Life Application Study Bible). I must say that the word *love* is so often confused by "sociality" nowadays.

You see, agape love, that is to say the God kind of love, is directed outward, toward others, and not inward, toward self. Some call it unconditional love, which is love without expecting anything back. Agape love is only possible with the help of God showing us how to set aside our own desires. The closer we come to Christ, the more love we will be able express toward others.

This brings me yet to another vital point that I want to share with you in this chapter of God's words of encouragement, and that is for you to come to know who you really are in Christ Jesus and walk in it. This is very important to your Christian walk and life. I am talking about your coming to understand your true identity of exactly who you really are as a believer in Him, so that no one can tell you different and that no devil in hell, as they say, can whisper you a lie! I was lead to meditate on this one day by the Spirit while I was doing my daily fellowship with Him in study. I put it this way because I truly understand that I can do nothing on my own. Jesus, while teaching his disciples, stated, "I am the vine; you are the branches. Those who remain in me, and I in them, will produce much fruit. For apart from me you can do nothing" (John 15:5). The entire chapter of John 15 is very uplifting, inspiring, assuring, and encouraging. Please take some quiet time alone with Him, reading and mediating His words.

Now back to who you really are in Christ Jesus and understanding your true identity. Here are twenty-five scriptural facts of who you really are in Christ as a believer. So study them and come to know them, and I challenge and dare you to walk in them believing them. You will see how greatly your life will begin to reform into that identity. Do it and see the anointed Word of God encourage you, strengthen you, and elevate you in Him, truly knowing and understanding who you are in Him. It goes for and above of you just being saved. God is good!!!

So are you ready to learn your true identity in Christ Jesus?

Romans 3:24
"Being justified freely by his grace through the redemption that is Christ Jesus . . ."

This means that we are declared "not guilty" of sin.

Romans 8:1-2
"There is therefore now no condemnation to them which are in Christ Jesus, who walk not after the flesh, but after the Spirit. For the law of the Spirit of life in Christ Jesus hath made me free from the law of sin and death."
This means that no condemnation is awaiting us.

1 Corinthians 1:2
"Unto the church of God which is at Corinth, to them that are sanctified in Christ Jesus, called to be saints, with all that in every place call upon the name of Jesus Christ our Lord, both their's and our's . . ."
This means we are acceptable to God through Jesus Christ.

1 Corinthians 1:30
"But of him are ye in Christ Jesus, who of God is made unto us wisdom, and righteousness, and sanctification, and redemption"
This means that we are made in Him pure and holy.

1 Corinthians 15:22
"For as in Adam all die, even so in Christ shall all be made alive."
This means we will rise again.

2 Corinthians 5:17
"Therefore if any man be in Christ, he is a new creature: old things are passed away; behold, all things are become new."
That means we are brand-new people inside.

2 Corinthians 5:21
"For he hath made him to be sin for us, who knew no sin: that we might be made the righteousness of God in him."
This means that we are made righteous in Christ when we trust in Him. Our sin was poured into Christ at His crucifixion, and His righteousness is poured into us at our conversion.

Galatians 3:28
"There is neither Jew nor Greek, there is neither bond nor free, there is neither male nor female: for ye are all one in Christ Jesus."
This means we are one in Christ Jesus with all believers.

Ephesians 1:3
"Blessed be the God and Father of our Lord Jesus Christ, who hath blessed us with all spiritual blessings in heavenly places in Christ."

This means we are blessed with every spiritual blessing in heaven.

Ephesians 1:4
"According as he hath chosen us in him before the foundation of
the world, that we should be holy and without blame
before him in love."

This means we are holy, faultless, and covered with God's love.

Ephesians 1:5-6
"Having predestinated us unto the adoption of children by Jesus
Christ to himself, according to the good pleasure of his will . . ."

This means we belong to Christ.

Ephesians 1:7
"In whom we have redemption through his blood, the forgiveness
of sins, according to the riches of his grace . . ."
This means our sins are taken away and are forgiven.

Ephesians 2:10
"For we are his workmanship, created in Christ Jesus unto good
works, which God hath before ordained that
we should walk in them."

This means we have been given new lives. We are his workmanship
created in Christ.

Ephesians 1:13
"In whom ye also trusted, after that ye heard the word of truth, the
gospel of your salvation: in whom also after that ye believed, ye
were sealed with that holy Spirit of promise."
This means are marked as belonging to God by the Holy Spirit."

Ephesians 2:6
"And hath raised us up together, and made us sit together in
heavenly places in Christ Jesus . . ."

This means we have been lifted from the grave to sit
with Christ in glory.

Ephesians 2:13
"But now in Christ Jesus ye who sometimes were far off are made
nigh by the blood of Christ."
This means we have been brought near to God.

Ephesians 3:6
"That the Gentiles should be fellowheirs, and of the same body, and
partakers of his promise in Christ by the gospel . . ."

This means we will receive great blessings.

Ephesians 3:12
"In whom we have boldness and access with confidence by the
faith of him . . ."

This means we can come fearlessly into the presence of God.

Ephesians 5:29-30

"For no man ever yet hated his own flesh; but nourisheth and
cherisheth it, even as the Lord the church: For we are members of
his body, of his flesh, and of his bones."

This means we are part of Christ's body, the church.

Colossians 2:10
"Ye are complete in him, which is the head of all
principality and power."

This means we are complete in Him, we have Christ,
and we are filled with God.

Colossians 2:11
"In whom also ye are circumcised with the circumcision made
without hands, in putting off the body of sins of the flesh by the
circumcision of Christ . . ."

This means we are set free from our evil desires.

2 Timothy 2:10
"Therefore I endure all things for the elect's sakes, that they may
also obtain the salvation which is in Christ Jesus
with eternal glory."

This means we have eternal glory.

Above, you have twenty-five Scriptures of who you are in Christ
Jesus. I encourage you to study them, come to know them, and live
them, because who you are in Him cannot be changed. The Bible
teaches us that there is nothing in all creation can ever separate us
from the love of God in Christ.

This is how our gracious God sees you in Christ. So come to know
this and believe this as you continue on your Christian journey. As
you do, I encourage you to live the following as well:

"Finally, my brethren, be strong in the Lord, and in the power of
his might. Put on the whole armour of God, that ye may be able to
stand against the wiles of the devil" (Ephesians 6:10-11). Why is this
so important? Because the Word of God tells us that "we wrestle not
against flesh and blood, but against principalities, against powers,
against the rulers of the darkness of this world, against spiritual
wickedness in high places" (Ephesians 6:12).

The Bible is telling us whom we are fighting against and to put on the
whole armor of God that we may be able to stand in the evil days.

If you have already given your life to Christ and are a church-going, Bible-believing, Bible–studying, and fellowshipping Christian, then you may have had the above Scripture taught and ministered to you many times. But for the sake of our babes in Christ and to further your understanding and to encourage you in this.

Let me break down what the whole armor of God is and how to use it property. We have been told so often that we must put on the whole armor of God, but we are hardly ever told or taught how to put on this armor or use it. I, being a retired army veteran, compare this to sending a soldier out to battle with his armor and weapon without ever telling or teaching him how to use them.

Throughout my Christian walk, from childhood to adulthood, from being a babe in Christ Jesus up to being a mature and maturing Christian, I have never seen or experienced being taught how to put on or use the whole armor of God, but only to just put it on.

But thanks be to God and to his unfailing Word that promises "the anointing will teach you all things without error" (. . .). It was how I came to understand this. By the reading of the Word, studying to show myself approve, and by the desire to understand this. Praise God!

Here is the whole (complete) armor of God as listed in Ephesians 6, and what we are to put on:

The truth . . . the breastplate of righteousness . . . our feet shod with the preparation of the gospel of peace . . . but above all, taking the shield of faith . . . the helmet of salvation . . . and the sword of the Spirit, which is the word of God.

But in doing we must pray always with all prayer and supplication in the Spirit, and watch thereunto with all perseverance and supplication for all saints.

To read and study it entirely, go to Ephesians 6:10-18, and pray asking God to give you a deep understanding pertaining to all that is stated there.

Personal notes:

Your Testimony

Here is the application of the whole armor of God:

Truth:
Satan fights with lies, and sometime his lies sound like the truth; but only believers have God's truth which can defeat Satan's lies. God's Word is true.

Breastplate:
Satan often attacks our hearts, which is the seat of our emotions and "self-worth," and God's approval is the breastplate that protects our hearts. He approves of us because he loves us and sent His Son to die for us on the cross.

Shod feet:
The readiness to spread the good news. Satan wants us to think that telling others about the good news of Jesus Christ is a worthless and hopeless task and a task too big, and that the negative responses are too much to bear. But the shoes God gives us are the motivation to continue with the great commission given to us by our Lord Jesus Christ to spread the good news that everyone needs to hear and know.

Shield of faith:
What we see are Satan's attacks in the form of insults, setbacks, and temptations. But the shield of faith protects us from Satan's flaming arrows that he shoots at us. But when we see as God sees, we go through our circumstances knowing that the ultimate victory is ours.

Helmet of salvation:
Satan wants to make us doubt God, Jesus, and salvation. The helmet protects our minds from doubting God's work he has done for us through Christ Jesus.

Sword of the Spirit:
The Word of God. The sword is our weapon of offense in putting
on the whole armor of God. When temptation comes, we need to
trust in the truth that is found in God's Word. And remember that
His word will never pass away, because He is His Word and He is
true!

We need to know all of the pieces of the armor of God and how to use
them and why, because we are engaged in a spiritual battle.

All believers find themselves subject to Satan's attacks because
they are no longer on his side, thus the apostle Paul in the book of
Ephesians tells us to put on the whole armor to resist Satan's attack
so that we can stand and stay true to God in the midst of them.

Lastly, I want you to picture the following as you read the Word of
God concerning putting on the whole armor of God. Picture a person
getting dressed for battle and putting on all that God told you to put
on in his Word.

Notice that He didn't give you a piece for the back. Why?

I can safely say that was so because He never meant for you to turn
around and run. The real battle is not yours, but His, and has already
been won! He has already conquered. He meant for us to go forward
into the victory that He has already given us in Christ Jesus.

Yes, know that the armor pieces listed are only symbolic. But the
weapons that they stand for are real and so is the spiritual war that
is mentioned in that same chapter.

Read the following verses and see what the Bible says about the
weapons that we have been given:

2 Corinthians 10:4-5
"(For the weapons of our warfare are not carnal [fleshy], but
mighty through God to the pulling down of strong holds;) Casting
down imaginations, and every high thing that exalteth itself

against the knowledge of God, and bringing into captivity every thought to the obedience of Christ . . ."

Ephesians 6:10
"Finally my brethren, be strong in the Lord, and in the power of his might."

In my studies, and putting this book together, I decided to keep it simple and did not change one letter of the written Word of God; for that would be a great sin.

Finally, I want you to know that if your heart is filled with the Word of God and if you diligently act on what God says and speak words of faith and not doubt, words of life and not death, words of victory and not defeat, you will walk in the victory that has been given to us all in Christ Jesus.

So lift your head up, gird up your loins, and shake yourself off! Then move forward in life with a purpose, knowing that God is with you always. He promises, as we have learned, that he will never leave you nor forsake you. He assured me personally while fallen under the power of the Spirit on January 21, 2005. I will go deeper into details in the following chapter. Believe in the promises of God and walk in them.

His words were:
"I am here; I never left you. If you believe in me, in my words, in my promises, just walk in them, for I have already given them to you."

He then charged me to "go tell my people. If they believe in me, in my words, in my promises, then just walk in them. I have already given it to them."

I share this with all of you whom the Lord has led and allowed to obtain a copy of this book to encourage you. There are many times that God has spoken a word in my spirit that lifted me up and encouraged me when I felt I couldn't go on. Many times in my life

I needed direction, encouragement, and strength. I found it in no other place more so than in the written Word of God.

His words are truly spirit and life, and food for our soul as well as health to our bodies. At this time, I want to give a personal word of encouragement to all, but especially to those who are called and were sent by God to do a chosen task, as well as to all who profess Christ Jesus. We should keep our life Christ-centered and not self-centered, job-centered, pastor-centered, or anything else. Please don't miss this. It is important to welcome Christ as the head of our life. We must allow His leadership in all areas of our life.

Now, having received salvation, the gift from God through his only begotten Son Jesus Christ; having the best gift ever given to you; having received the eternal gift of salvation from the divine heavenly Father, know that with this gift come promises, promises that you can stand on without wondering if they will be kept. Assured that His words will last forever, you can hold these promises to heart, knowing that they have been and will be fulfilled.

Your salvation, which came through Jesus Christ, is a gift from God and gives you eternal life the moment that you accept Jesus in to your heart as your personal Lord and Savior. Your eternal life begins right then, not when you get to heaven. You have a secure place in heaven with our heavenly Father. How can I say this with such certainty? How can it be you asked? Jesus said, "In my Father's house are many mansions: if it were not so, I would have told you. I go to prepare a place for you. And if I go and prepare a place for you, I will come again, and receive you unto myself; that where I am, there ye may be also" (John 14:2-3).

To God be the glory! There you have it, right from the very mouth of the One who saved you; the One whose blood was shed; the One who was crucified, buried, and raised alive—the very One who stands at the right hand of the Father in heaven, advocating for us, saying, "My blood was shed for him; my body was beaten and bruised for her." We have an eternal place in the heaven of heavens. Yet there are other promises, like those of Psalm 91. It's an awesome psalm to read and mediate on, knowing that Jesus Christ is your personal Lord and Savior. Just for a moment, I want to draw your complete attention to these particular verses of that psalm. Please read Psalm 91:14-16 and pay close attention to who is making these promises. "Because he hath set his love upon me, therefore will I deliver him: I will set him on high, because he hath known my name. He shall call upon me, and I will answer him: I will be with him in trouble; I will deliver him, and honour him. With long life will I satisfy him, and shew him my salvation."

Did you catch that? Read the entire psalm, and you'll know who that "I" is referring to. God is good! The Holy Bible is full of the promises of God to you and me. Yes, they come with conditions, but you've met these conditions through Jesus Christ. No, not from what we have done. There is nothing that any of us from the creation of time as we know it to this present date in time could have done, but because of what Jesus Christ has done, Jesus the only begotten Son of the Father.

When John was baptizing Jesus in the Jordan River, God said, "This is my beloved Son, in whom I am well pleased" (Matthew 4:17). We, being children of the King, sons and daughters of God, have His promises and blessings that come with knowing Jesus as personal Lord and Savior. Before I go on into the promises of God, I want to show you scripturally that we are sons and daughters of God, children of the King Jesus Christ. Romans 8:14: "For as many as are led by the Spirit of God, they are the sons of God."

Romans 8:16: "The Spirit itself beareth witness with our spirit, that we are the children of God."

Scripture didn't stop there. Let's read on. Romans 8:17: "And if children, then heirs; heirs of God, and joint-heirs with Christ; if so be that we suffer with him, that we may be also glorified together."

APPLICATION WORK SHEET

Let's recap so that when the time comes for you to gird up your
loins and put on your whole armor of God daily,
you know that the time is now!

[Without looking at the other page, see if you can write out the
application of each piece of spiritual armor.]

- Truth: _____
  _____
  _____.

- Breastplate: _____
  _____
  _____.

- Shod feet: _____
  _____
  _____.

- Shield of faith: _____
  _____
  _____.

- Helmet of salvation: _____
  _____
  _____.

- Sword of the Spirit: _____
  _____
  _____.

CHAPTER 15

BELIEVE IN THE PROMISES OF GOD AND WALK IN THEM

We, the saints, must know that we serve an awesome God who has all power. We must know and believe that God cannot lie or fail! It's impossible for Him, because when He made His promises, there was no one else to swear by—He swore by Himself. We must know that whatever God has spoken will come to pass. All we have to do is just walk in it, receiving it by faith, for He has already worked it out for us through Jesus Christ, our blessed Savior. It's now time for us, the saints of God, to come the realization of the promises of our God. He said point-blank,

> If you believe in me (in my word, in my promises),
> just walk in them!

In John 14:1, Jesus said, "Let not your heart be troubled: ye believe in God, believe also in me." Activate your faith; move out on the things of God and all that He has promised in His Holy Word. He said, "Till heaven and earth pass, one jot or one tittle shall in no wise pass from the law, till all be fulfilled" (Matthew 5:18).

What a promise and what assurance! You should feel and comfort to know that heaven and earth will pass away before He changes or goes back on His Word. And within His Word are all the blessings and promises He has given us and will give us.

Think about it; this includes healing, deliverance, salvation, and His divine protection. His Word says that He will never leave us or forsake us. (Hebrews 13:5) What more assurance do we need to believe that all we have to do is just believe and accept His Word as faithful and true.

The Holy Bible tells us that He is His Word and that He is true. Scripture teaches us that "God is a Spirit: and they that worship him must worship him in spirit and in truth" (John 4:24).

Jesus Christ, our Lord and Savior, said, making it undeniably clear, that He alone is the Way, the Truth, and the Life, and that no one can come to the Father but by Him. (John 14:6)

Within the promises of God, he said, "When thou passest through the waters, I will be with thee; and through the rivers, they shall not overflow thee: when thou walkest through the fire, thou shalt not be burned; neither shall the flame kindle upon thee" (Isaiah 43:2). If you've found salvation through his Son Jesus Christ, this, too, is promised to you. Let me remind you of the three Hebrew boys who were faithful to God. They didn't just walk through the fire. They walked all around in it and were not burned. What a promise of God!

God's promises are real; He takes care of His children. Come to know Him as Abba; come to know Jesus as your personal Lord and Savior. Come to know who you are in Him. Believe in the promises of God and walk in them. He also said that by the stripes of His dear Son, you are healed. Saints of God, the hindrance of the promises of God in one's live is not on Him.

It is solely based on whether we believe in the promises. Do we believe in Him? Hebrews 11:6: "But without faith it is impossible to please him: for he that cometh to God must *believe* that he is, and that he is a rewarder of them that diligently seek him" (my italics).

John 3:16: "For God so loved the world, that he gave his only begotten Son, that whosoever *believeth* in him should not perish, but have everlasting life" (my italics). Scripture goes on and on about having to believe. God gave us His best. He gave His only Son. Jesus did it all and took it all for us. All you and I have to do is just believe, receive, and act on it. When Jesus said that it was finished, He meant it all was finished. He did everything that one will ever have to do to be saved and to receive the blessings and the promises of God. But there was something that that even He couldn't to for you and me, and that is to believe. God did is part by sending his Son Jesus, who was faithful and obedient to the will of his Father, to suffer and die on the cross.

Someone reading this book may be thinking, *I through this was to be about the promises of God.* Well, if you know your Old Testament, you will know and understand that Jesus Christ is the promise seed of God.

As I said earlier, Scripture teaches us that without faith, it is impossible to please God, and that those who come to Him must believe that He is. This tells me that we must have faith, believe, and then act on what we believe. This leads me to this question: Why are many Christians not seeing the manifestation of the promises of God in their lives? It can't be because they don't have faith. The Bible says that we all have been given a measure of faith. (Romans 12:3) The Bible also tells us that Jesus Christ is the author and finisher of our faith.

I lay the question before you once again: Where is the hindrance in us not to receive the promises of God? I believe the answer to this question is our believing. You have Christians that profess Christ Jesus and yet don't believe—carnal Christians, believing by sight and not by faith. We as followers of Jesus Christ must walk by faith and not by sight.

Now I will repeat the words that the Lord spoke to me on January 21, 2005, as I was caught up in the spirit. He said, "I am here. I never left you. If you believe in me, in my word, in my promises, then walk in them. I have already given them to you." Then he said, "Go, tell my people that if they believe in me, in my word, in my promises.

Just walk in them. I have already given it to them. You have been charged."

I share what God said because it is the reason for this chapter. God already gave; we must receive. Jesus already did the work; now we must believe and walk in all that came with our salvation. Let us understand that when our awesome God speaks, he speaks in the right, the present, tense. Plainly put, God speaks in the now tense. We are the ones who are waiting on the manifestation to come to pass. We have to live a faith walker style of life, lining up with the Word of God.

In His holy Word, He said that my word will not return to me void, but will accomplish the purpose in which it was sent. (Isaiah 55:11) He also spoke to me in my earlier Christian life while in Sunday morning service. He said, "My Word! My Word! Put your mind on my Word. Look at my Word again! I watch over my Word to see that it come to pass!"

That right there has strengthened my walk with Him since then to this very day. My entire life has been affected and changed because of my belief in the Word of God. I truly understand now for many reasons why our Lord Jesus Christ said, "Man shall not live by bread alone, but by every word that proceedeth out of the mouth of God" (Matthew 4:4).

His speaking those words in my spirit and my believing and receiving them in my heart, encouraged me to continue running the race, while holding on to His Word, believing in the promises. He actually spoke those words into my spirit as He so stated in the Holy Bible. We as believers should grasp ahold of that and never let go, knowing that He will hold us up in the midst of the waters; and it doesn't matter whether we know how to swim or not. He has promised not to let us drown. What a mighty God we serve! Such love and compassion that he held nothing back from us! He stepping out of heaven to walk the land, make away for the entire world of all the "Whosoevers."

But if we only believe and walk in his promises. Now let's talk about what it means to believe. Webster's dictionary gives the definition for *believe* as follows: "1; to take as true, real etc. 2; to have confidence in a statement or promise of (another person) 3; to suppose or think—vi 2; to have religious faith."

Having a clear understanding of what the word *believe* means, we must also well understand the biblical fact that our faith and belief must work together. I say this because it is possible for one to believe in something but have no faith in it. Let me share with you Hebrews 4:1-4: "Let us therefore fear, lest, a promise being left us of entering into his rest, any of you should seem to come short of it. For unto us was the gospel preached, as well as unto them: but the word preached did not profit them, not being mixed with faith in them that heard it. For we which have believed do enter into rest, as he said."

James 2:17 says, "Faith, if it hath not works, is dead." If you searched the Scriptures, you would notice throughout Jesus' earthly ministry, He went about preaching, teaching, healing, delivering, and setting the captives free. You would notice where He stated quite often in every incident, "Your faith has made you whole." Another place in Scripture records that when Jesus went to His hometown, He could do only little work because of the people's unbelief. The Bible said that He marveled at their unbelief. He was and is the King of Kings. See how important it is for one to believe in the promise to receive, and walk in them. The point is that Jesus knew that we must believe in order to receive promises of God.

The woman with the issue of blood had faith and believed in her heart that if she could just push her way through the crowd and touch the hem of Jesus' garment, she would be healed. And when she did, she was healed. And if we have studied our Bibles or have heard the message preached, we know that Jesus turned and found the woman after seeking her when she fell at His feet. He said, "Woman, your faith has made you whole. Go in peace."

God is Good and True to His Word

God's promises bring contentment in every situation. The apostle Paul said in Philippians 4:11, "For I have learned, in whatsoever state I am, therewith to be content." The focus here is to learn to rely on God's promises and Christ's strength to help you to be content. The point that I am bringing out here is whatever state you may be in or facing, rely on God's Word believing in His promises concerning it.

We must remember that a promise is only as good as the person who is making it. We who believe and know that God is good, all-powerful, all-knowing, everywhere at once, and as he placed in my spirit one day while studying His Word, all-perfect!

So we can stand on His Word, believing in His promises. Every guarantee comes with conditions, and so do the promises of God. What are the conditions? They were shared in the first part of this book. We must first realize the fact that we were lost in sin, destined for hell, and in need of a Savior. What am I saying? I am saying that we must come to know Jesus Christ as Lord and Savior, believing that He died for our sins, was raised from the dead by the Spirit of God, and is right now at the right hand of the Father in heaven. But it doesn't stop there; we must continue to strive to live the life of that which we profess as Christians.

And Jesus, the author and finisher of our faith, did not leave us alone: "And I will pray the Father, and he shall give you another Comforter, that he may abide with you for ever" (John 14:16).

"I will not leave you comfortless; I will come to you" (John 14:18). Remember the earlier parts of this book where it was shared with you what Romans 8:14 states: "For as many as are led by the Spirit of God, they are the sons of God."

It is important to learn about God's promises in the Bible.

In knowing that his promises will be fulfilled according to his timetable, not ours. When we learn of those promises, the ones that have already come to pass, trusting God that He is able to bring all promises to pass would help us. It is easy to become impatient, wanting God to act right now in certain situations. But we should continue in the faith, knowing that God will always keep his promises. A promise from God is a sure thing, no matter how unlikely it may seem. Remember, what is impossible with man, is possible with God. And please don't forget this: "God word isn't subject to majority opinions." Please let us never forget that God's truth is set apart from feelings, situations, or opinions.

In Numbers, Caleb stood for the truth. He knew about God, apart from what he saw. He knew that God's promises could be depended on. God said plainly that He would help them conquer the Promised Land. We should believe and move out on the promises of God in spite of others' opinions.

Just a brief word to those who make promises to God in prayer: Know that it is dishonest and dangerous to ignore a promise, especially to God. The bottom line concerning this is God keeps His promises and He expects you to keep yours. Know that God always fulfills His promises at the right time. God knows when to act. When you feel that God has forgotten you in your troubles, just remember that God has a time schedule we can't see. He says in his Word, "For my thoughts are not your thoughts, neither are your ways my ways" (Isaiah 55:8). A personal insight on weathering the storms of life: Try focusing on the promise and not on the problem. Trust Him to bring it to pass.

To walk in the promises of God, you must move out in faith. Remember, without faith it is impossible to please Him. What is faith? Hebrews 11:1 says, "Now faith is the substance of things hoped for, the evidence of things not seen." I want to break the word *faith* down by letters:

F = faithfulness

A = anointed

I = inward led

T = trustworthy and testimony

H = heirs of God

There's that word again, "Faith."

Faith is the key that unlocks the door. Let me take it little farther concerning walking in the promises of God by faith. Remember, faith is now, hope is the future. Faith is taking God at His Word. Faith has nothing to do with our five senses. Faith is based on what God says about the situation. Faith is what moves God. The beginning of faith is believing in God's character, believing in who He says He is, and believing that there is no other like Him and that He will do what He says that He will do.

When we believed that God will fulfill His promises even though we don't see those promises manifesting yet, we demonstrate true faith. The law of faith mandates that we believe God even if we die before He delivers His promises. Why? If you haven't figure it out yet from studying, reading , and hearing the gospel of Jesus Christ, death itself couldn't hold Jesus in the grave. That's right, even death cannot stop the promises of God. We are called to walk by faith and not by sight.

There is something else we need to learn about faith, and that is speaking by faith is not lying. A lie is meant to deceive someone; it is designed to make someone believe something that is not true. Know this, speaking by faith is simply agreeing with the Word of God. Faith is now, hope is the future. But to have hope is not a bad thing either, according to Scripture.

It is important to remember that spiritual things are not based on feelings but on faith. Faith doesn't deny reality, but faith, as we have learned, is speaking as though it were so. I am not talking "name it and claim it" here. Let me give two more points concerning faith and walking in the promises of God. First, don't speak what you see and feel. Speak what you believe, and that should be what's in the Word of God. Jesus said that we should live by every word that should proceed out the mouth of God. Second, we should act on God's Word before we see any change in our circumstance, while our situation remains the same. The Word of God tells us, "So as a man think, there so he is." To put it plainly, you're what you think.

God's Word has awesome power, and I want to once again pause right here and restate a biblical fact concerning the Word of God: "For the word of God is quick, and powerful, and sharper than any twoedged sword, piercing even to the dividing asunder of soul and spirit, and of the joints and marrow, and is a discerner of the thoughts and intents of the heart" (Hebrews 4:12).

We are walking by faith when our confidence is in Him, knowing that He is able to keep his promises. Faith is a very powerful force; it is a creative force. It must be put into action. Faith must be released in order to work. It takes faith to move the hands of God. According to the written Word of God, it's impossible to please Him without it. Now let's gird up our loins and move out in faith, as we believe and walk in the promises of God.

Now Is the Time to Rise Up and Not Give Up, but Believe

The book of Titus says, "My people are dying because of the lack of knowledge of me." So search the Scriptures and come to know all God's promises to you. The Bible is filled with them, and so, within this last chapter, I will share with you sixty-six areas in which some of the promises of God you should know as a child of God, joint heirs in Christ Jesus that is given unto you. Come to know them, rise up from where you are, and walk in these promises of God.

Now believing and walking in these particular sixty-six promises of our God that have been given for our lives has encouraged my personal Christian walk. Since I started this journey with Him, even as I paused and looked back, I have been convinced without the slightest doubt that God truly watches over His Word to see that it comes to pass. And I know without a doubt that if you, too, only believe and just walk in His promises, and be not moved, you will find that your personal Christian walk with Him will be full of assurance, because you will not be walking it alone.

You will be walking by faith, and that pleases Him. What child doesn't want to please his or her father? And what father is not pleased when his children walk in obedience to his word. To God be the glory!

Sixty-six Promises of God to Rise Up and Walk In

- Abuse
- Abuse of substance
- Adversity
- Anger
- Anointing
- Anxiety
- Appearance
- Attitude
- Balance
- Bitterness
- Career
- Change
- Character
- Choices
- Comfort
- Communication
- Conflict
- Conscience
- Courage
- Dating and marriage
- Depression
- Destiny

- Direction
- Discouragement
- Emotions
- Eternal life
- Failure
- Faith
- Family
- Fear
- Finances
- Forgiveness
- God's Word
- Grief
- Guidance
- Guilt
- Healing
- Health
- Hearing God's voice
- Honesty
- Hope
- Humility
- Joy
- Keeping promises
- Love
- Money
- Obedience
- Patience
- Peace
- Perseverance
- Praise and worship
- Prayer
- Prosperity
- Repentance
- Restoration
- Seeking God's face
- Self-control

- Self-esteem (see also chapter 14)
- Spiritual growth
- Stress
- Suffering
- Talents
- Temptations
- Trust
- Unity
- Wisdom

ABUSE

"He delivers me from enemies; you also lift me above those who rise against me; You have delivered me from the violent man. Therefore I will give thanks to you, O Lord."
Psalm 18:48-49

"You are my hiding place; you shall preserve me from trouble; you shall surround me about with songs of deliverance."
Psalm 32:7 (KJ2000)

"Before I formed you in the womb I knew you; Before you were born I sanctified you."
Jeremiah 1:5 (NKJV)

ABUSE OF SUBSTANCE

"Do not get drunk on wine, which leads to debauchery. Instead, be filled with the Spirit."
Ephesians 5:18 (NIV)

"Woe to those who rise early in the morning to run after their drinks, who stay up late at night till they are inflamed with wine."
Isaiah 5:11-12 (NIV)

"Who has woe? Who has sorrow? Who has strife? Who has complaints? Who has needless bruises? Who has bloodshot eyes? Those who linger over wine, who go to sample bowls of mixed wine. Do not gaze at wine when it is red, when it sparkles in the cup, when it goes down smoothly! In the end it bites like a snake and poisons like a viper. Your eyes will see strange sights, and your mind will imagine confusing things. You will be like one sleeping on the high seas, lying on top of the rigging. 'They hit me,' you will say, 'but I'm not hurt! They beat me, but I don't feel it! When will I wake up so I can find another drink?'"
Proverbs 23:29-35 (NIV)

"Don't you know that you yourselves are God's temple and that God's Spirit dwells in your midst? If anyone destroys God's temple, God will destroy that person; for God's temple is sacred, and you together are that temple."
1 Corinthians 3:16-17 (NIV)
(Assurance plus a word of warning, yet with love.
Please don't take this lightly. God means what he said.)

ADVERSITY

I closed this book, *Salvation: A Gift From God*, God's word of encouragement. Believe in the promises of God and walk in them, with the prophetic words of our Lord which He spoke into our lives. To those who know that you are called of the Lord to work in the vineyard.
Please read the next page, praying asking God to give you complete understanding concerning this so that you would not lean on your own understanding, but consider this as assurance in which we can stand on and walk in.

"No, in all these things we are more than conquerors through him who loved us. For I am convinced that neither death nor life, neither angels nor demons, neither the present nor the future,

nor any powers, neither height nor depth, nor anything else in all creation, will be able to separate us from the love of God that is in Christ Jesus our Lord."
Romans 8:37-39 (NIV)

"Have I not commanded you? Be strong and courageous. Do not be afraid; do not be discouraged, for the Lord your God will be with you wherever you go."
Joshua 1:9 (NIV)

"For whoever is born of God overcomes the world: and this is the victory that overcomes the world, even our faith."
1 John 5:4 (KJ2000)

"Beloved, do not think it is strange concerning the fiery trial which is to try you, as though some strange thing happened to you; but rejoice to the extent that you partake of Christ's suffering, that when His glory is revealed, you may also be glad with exceeding joy."
1 Peter 4:12-13

"But he knows the way that I take; when he has tested me, I will come forth as gold."
Job 23:10 (NIV)

"The righteous cry out, and the Lord hears, And delivers them out of all their troubles."
Psalm 34:17 (NKJV)

"When you pass through the waters, I will be with you; and through the rivers, they shall not overwhelm you; when you walk through fire you shall not be burned, and the flame shall not consume you. For I am the Lord your God."
Isaiah 43:2-3 (ESV)

A Devotional Thought to Meditate On

Don't be discouraged by adversity. The purpose for which God created you is worth the struggle. Keep on trusting Him. Keep on living by the principles of love in which He has written His Word. So don't give in to peer pressure; give in to God.

ANGER

"My dear brothers and sisters, take note of this: Everyone should be quick to listen, slow to speak and slow to become angry, because human anger does not produce the righteousness that God desires."
James 1:19-20 (NIV)

"Cease from anger, and forsake wrath;
Do not fret—it only causes harm."
Psalm 37:8 (NKJV)

"Do not hasten in your spirit to be angry, For anger rests in the bosom of fools."
Ecclesiastes 7:9 (NKJV)

"Starting a quarrel is like breaching a dam; so drop the matter before a dispute breaks out."
Proverbs 17:14 (NIV)

"'In your anger do not sin': Do not let the sun go down while you are still angry, and do not give the devil a foothold."
Ephesians 4:26-27 (NIV)

"Beloved, do not avenge yourselves, but rather give place to wrath; for it is written, 'Vengeance is Mine, I will repay,' says the Lord."
Romans 12:19 (NKJV)

ANOINTING

"You have the anointing of the Holy One,
and you know all things."
1 John 2:20

"But the anointing which you have received from Him abides in
you, and you do not need that anyone teach you; but as the same
anointing teaches you concerning all things, and is true, and is not
a lie, and just as it has taught you, will abide in Him."
1 John 2:27

"He who establishes us with in Christ and has anointed us is God,
who also has sealed us and given us the Spirit
in our hearts as a guarantee."
1 Corinthians 1:21-22

ANXIETY

"Jesus said, 'Do not let your hearts be troubled.
Ye, trust in God; trust also in me.'"
John 14:1

"Therefore do not worry about tomorrow, for tomorrow will worry
about itself. Each day has enough trouble of its own"
Matthew 6:25-34 (NIV)

APPEARANCE

"Your beauty should not come from outward adornment, such
as braided hair and the wearing of gold jewelry and fine clothes.
Instead, it should be that of your inner self, the unfading beauty of
a gentle and quiet spirit, which is of great worth in God's sight."
1 Peter 3:3-4 (NIV)

"God spoke to Samuel saying, 'The Lord does not look at the things
man looks at: Man looks at the outward appearance,
but the Lord looks at the heart.'"
1 Samuel 6:7

ATTITUDE

"And let us not grow weary while doing good, for in due
season we shall reap if we do not lose heart."
Galatians 6:9 (NKJV)

"Let your conduct be without covetousness; be content with such
things as you have. For He Himself has said, 'I will never leave you
nor forsake you.' So we may boldly say: 'The Lord is my helper; I
will not fear. What can man do to me?'"
Hebrews 13:5-6 (NKJV)

"Cast your burden on the Lord, And He shall sustain you; He shall
never permit the righteous to be moved."
Psalm 55:22 (NKJV)

"Whatever you do, whether in word or deed, do it all in the name
of the Lord Jesus, giving thanks to God the Father through him."
Colossians 3:17 (NIV)

"Jesus taught them saying, 'Be merciful just as your Father is
merciful. Do not judge; and you will not be judged. Do not
condemn, and you will not be condemned. Forgive ,
and you will be forgiven.'"
Luke 6:36-37

"Do not think of yourself more highly than you ought, but think
of yourself with sober judgment, in accordance with the measure
of faith God has given you. Hate what is evil; cling to what is good.
Be devoted to one another in brotherly love. Honor one another

above yourselves. Never be lacking in zeal, but keep your spiritual fervor, serving the Lord. Be joyful in hope, patient in affliction, faithful in prayer. Share with God's people who are in need. Pratice hospitality. Bless those who persecute you; bless and do not curse. Rejoice with those who rejoice; mourn with those mourn. Live in harmony with one another."
Romans 12:3, 9-16

BALANCE

"A man's heart plans his way, but the Lord directs his steps."
Proverbs 16:9 (KJ2000)

"For the ways of a man are before the eyes of the Lord, And He watches all his paths."
Proverbs 5:21 (NASB)

"Restore me to the joy of your salvation, and uphold me by your generous Spirit."
Psalm 51:12

BITTERNESS

"Looking carefully lest anyone fall short of the grace of God; lest any root of bitterness springing up cause trouble, and by this many become defiled."
Hebrews 12:15 (NKJV)

"If you have bitter envy and self-seeking in your hearts, do not boast and lie against the truth. This wisdom does not descend from above, but is earthly, sensual, demonic."
James 3:14-15 (NKJV)

CAREER

"I am the Lord your God who teaches you to profit,
who leads you by the way that you should go."
Isaiah 48:17 (KJ2000)

"You shall remember, the Lord your God, for it is He who gives you
power to get wealth that he may establish his covenant, with he
swore to your fathers, as it is today."
Deuteronomy 8:18

"Through wisdom a house is built, And by understanding it is
established; By knowledge the rooms are filled
With all precious and pleasant riches."
Proverbs 24:3-4 (NKJV)

CHANGE

"Therefore if anyone is in Christ, he is a new creature; the old
things passed away; behold, new things have come."
2 Corinthians 5:17 (NASB)

"Do not remember the former things, Nor consider the things of
old. Behold, I will do a new thing, Now it shall spring forth; Shall
you not know it? I will even make a road in the
wilderness And rivers in the desert."
Isaiah 43: 18-19 (NKJV)

"But one thing I do, forgetting those things which are behind and
reaching forward to those things which are ahead, I press toward
the goal for the prize of the upward call of God in Christ Jesus."
Philippians 3:13-14 (NKJV)

CHARACTER

"But as he who called you is holy, you also be
holy in all your conduct."
1 Peter 1:15 (ESV)

"Let us purify ourselves from everything that contaminates body
and spirit, perfecting holiness out of reverence for God."
2 Corinthians 7:1 (NIV)

"Then the Lord said to Satan, 'Have you considered my servant
Job? There is no one on earth like him; he is blameless and upright,
a man who fears God and shuns evil. And he still maintains his
integrity, though you incited me against him
to ruin him without any reason.'"
Job 2:3 (NIV)

"A truthful witness gives honest testimony, but
a false witness tells lies."
Proverbs 12:17 (NIV)

CHOICES

"Jesus said, 'I have set you an example that you
should do as I have done.'"
John 13:15

COMFORT

"Let not your heart be troubled: you believe in God,
believe also in me."
John 14:1 (KJ2000)

"He heals the brokenhearted And binds up their wounds."
Psalm 147:3 (NASB)

"Blessed are those who mourn, for they shall be comforted."
Matthew 5:4 (ESV)

A Devotional Thought to Meditate On

For God has said, "I will never leave you, I will not forsake you. I will be with you even unto the end of the world."

COMMUNICATION

"Let no corrupt words proceed out of your mouth, but what is good for edification, that it may impart grace to the hearers."
Ephesians 4:29

"A soft answer turns away wrath, but a harsh word stirs up anger. The tongue of the wise uses knowledge rightly."
Proverb 15:1-2

"But avoid foolish disputes, genealogies, contentions, and strivings about the law; for they are unprofitable and useless."
Titus 3:9 (NKJV)

"But for every idle word men speak, they shall give account of it in the day of judgment."
Matthew 12:36

CONFLICT

"Jesus taught them saying, 'If your brother sins against you, go and show him his fault just between the two of you. If he listens to you, you have won your brother over. But if he will not listen, take one or two other along, so that every matter may be established by the

testimony of two or three witness. If he refuses to listen to them, tell the church, treat him as you would a pagan or tax collector.'"
Matthew 18:15-17

CONSCIENCE

"Jesus said, 'I will as the Father, and he will give you another Counselor to be with you forever, the Spirit of truth. When he comes, he will convict the world of guilt in regard to sin.'"
John 14:16; 16-8

"Jesus replied, 'Your Father sees what is done in secret.'"
Matthew 6:4

COURAGE

"Wait on the Lord; be of good courage, and he shall strengthen your heart; Wait, I say on the Lord."
Psalm 27:14

"Watch, stand fast in the faith, be brave, be strong. Let all that you do be done with love."
1 Corinthians 16:13 (NKJV)

"The Lord is faithful, who shall establish you, and guard you from the evil one."
2 Thessalonians 3:3 (ASV)

"The Lord will be your confidence and will keep your foot from being caught."
Proverbs 3:26 (ESV)

"The Lord is good, a stronghold in the day of trouble; he knows those who take refuge in him."
Nahum 1:7 (ESV)

DATING AND MARRIAGE

"Do not be yoked together with unbelievers. For what do righteousness and wickedness have in common? Or what fellowship can light have with darkness?"
2 Corinthians 6:14 (NIV)

"A good wife or husband will either make or break their life. Her duties lay the foundation for her family's welfare."
Proverbs 31-1031

DEPRESSION

"In the world you will have tribulation. But take heart;
I have overcome the world."
John 16:33 (ESV)

"Weeping may endure for a night, but joy comes in the morning."
Psalm 30:5 (KJ2000)

"He heals the brokenhearted And binds up their wounds."
Psalm 147:3 (NASB)

"We also glory in tribulations, knowing that tribulation produces perseverance; and perseverance, character; and character, hope. Now, hope does not disappoint, because the love of God has been poured out in our hearts by the Holy Spirit who was given to us."
Romans 5:3-5

DESTINY

"For I know the thoughts that I think towards you, said the Lord, thoughts of peace, and not of evil, to give you an expected end."
Jeremiah 29:11

"Eye has not seen, nor ear heard, Nor have entered into the heart of man The things which God has prepared for those who love Him."
1 Corinthians 2:9 (NKJV)

DIRECTION

"If any of you lacks wisdom, let him ask God, who gives to all liberally and without reproach, and it will be given to him."
James 1:5

"I will instruct you and teach you in the way you should go; I will guide you with my eye."
Psalm 32:8

"The steps of a good man are ordered by the Lord, and he delights in his ways."
Psalm 37:23

"When the Spirit of truth comes, he will guide you into all the truth, for he will not speak on his own authority, but whatever he hears he will speak, and he will declare to you the things that are to come."
John 16:13 (ESV)

DISCOURAGEMENT

"God is my strength and power: and he makes my way perfect."
2 Samuel 22:23 (KJ2000)

"He that dwelleth in the secret place of the most High shall abide under the shadow of the Almighty. I will say of the Lord, He is my refuge and my fortress: my God; in him will I trust."
Psalm 91:1-2

EMOTIONS

"For we do not have a High Priest who cannot sympathize with our weakness, but was in all points tempted as we are, yet without sin. Let us therefore come boldly to the throne of grace, that we may obtain mercy, and find grace to help in time of need."
Hebrews 4:15-16

"For you, Lord, have made me glad through your work: I will triumph in the works of your hands."
Psalm 92:4 (KJ2000)

ENCOURAGEMENT

"Let us hold unwavingly to the hope we profess, for God who promised is faithful. And let us consider how we may spur one another on toward love and good deeds. Let us not give up meeting together, as same are in the habit of doing, but let us encourage one another and all the more as you see the day approaching."
Hebrews 10:23-25

"Encourage one another daily, as long as it is called Today."
Hebrews 3:13 (NIV)

"For everything that was written in the past was written to teach us, so that through endurance and the encouragement of the Scriptures we might have hope."
Romans 15:4 (NIV)

ETERNAL LIFE

"God has given us eternal life and this is in his Son. He who has the Son has life; he who does not have the Son of God does not

have life. I write these things to you who believe in the name of the Son of God so that you may know that you have eternal life."
1 John 5:11-13

"Jesus said, 'I am the resurrection and the life. He who believes in me will live, even though he dies; and whoever lives and believes in me will never die.'"
John 11:25-26

FAILURE

"Jesus replied, 'watch and pray so that you will not fall into temptation. The spirit is willing, but the body is weak.'"
Matthew 26:41

"If anyone be in Christ, he is a new creation; the old has gone, the new has come!"
2 Corinthians 5:17

"There is therefore now no condemnation to those who are in Christ Jesus, who do not walk according to the flesh, but according to the Spirit."
Romans 8: 1 (NKJV)

"Surely goodness and mercy shall follow me all the days of my life, and I shall dwell in the house of the Lord forever."
Psalm 23:6 (ESV)

FAITH

"Because you have seen me, you have believed: blessed are they that have not seen, and yet have believed."
John20:24-29 (KJ2000)

"We live by faith, not by sight."
2 Corinthians 5:7 (NIV)

"Without faith it is impossible to please God, because anyone who
comes to him must believe that he exists and that he
rewards those who earnestly seek him."
Hebrews 11:6 (NIV)

"By grace you have been saved through faith, and that not of
yourselves; it is the gift of God, not of works,
that no one would boast."
Ephesians 2:8-9 (WEB)

"So then faith comes by hearing, and hearing by the word of God."
Romans 10:17 (KJ2000)

FAMILY

"If you're a Christian, you definitely have a responsibility to make
every effort to resolve conflicts in a peaceful manner and avoid
them whenever possible."
Genesis 31:19-20

"Believe on the Lord Jesus Christ, and you will be saved,
you and your household."
Acts 16:31 (NKJV)

"Above all love each other deeply, because love
covers over a multitude of sins."
1 Peter 4:8 (NIV)

FEAR

"God has not given us a spirit of fear, but of power and
of love and of a sound mind."
2 Timothy 1:7 (NKJV)

"So, we may boldly say; 'The Lord is my helper, I will not fear.
What can man do to me.'"
Hebrews 13:6

"There is no fear in love; but perfect love casts our fear, because
fear involves torment. But he who fears has not been
made perfect in love."
1 John 4:18

"I sought the Lord, and he heard me, and delivered me,
from all my fears."
Psalm 34: 4

"Yea, though I walk through the valley of the shadow of death, I
will fear no evil: for thou art with me; thy rod and
thy staff, they comfort me."
Psalm 23:4 (Darby)

FINANCES

"My God shall supply all your needs according to his
riches in glory by Christ Jesus."
Philippians 4:19

"The Lord will grant you plenty of goods, in the fruit of your
body, in the increase of your livestock, and in the produce of
your ground, in the land of which the Lord swore to your fathers
to give you. The Lord will open to you His good treasure, the
heavens, to give the rain to your land in its season, and to bless all
the work of your hand. You shall lend to many nations, but you

shall not borrow. And the Lord will make you the head and not the tail; you shall be above only, and not be beneath, if you heed the commandments of the Lord your God, which I command you today, and are careful to observe them."
Deuteronomy 28:11-13 (NKJV)

"Give, and it will be given to you: good measure, pressed down, shaken together, and running over, will be given to you. For with the same measure you measure it will be measured back to you."
Luke 6:38 (WEB)

"But this says: He who sows sparingly will also reap sparingly, and he who sows bountifully will also reap bountifully. So let each one give as he purposes in his heart, not grudgingly. Or of necessity; for God loves a cheerful giver. And God is able to make all grace abound toward you, that you always having all sufficiency in all things, may have an abundance for every good work."
2 Corinthians 9:6-8

FORGIVENESS

"If we confess our sins, he is faithful and just will forgive us our sins and purify us from all unrighteousness."
1 John 1:9

"In Him we have redemption through His blood, the forgiveness of sins, according to the riches of His grace."
Ephesians 1:7 (NKJV)

"I will be merciful to their unrighteousness, and their sins and their lawless deeds I will remember no more."
Hebrews 8:12 (NKJV)

"If you forgive men their trespasses, your Heavenly Father will also forgive you. But if you do not forgive men their trespasses, Neither will your Father forgive your trespasses."
Matthew 6:14-15

GOD'S WORD

"The word of God is quick, and powerful, sharper then a two-edged sword."
Hebrews 4:12

GRIEF

"Fear not, for I am with you; be not dismayed, for I am your God; I will strengthen you, I will help you, I will uphold you with my righteous right hand."
Isaiah 41:10 (ESV)

"O' death, where is your sting? O' hades, where is your victory? The sting of death is sin, and the strength of sin is the law. But thanks be to God, who gives us the victory through our Lord Jesus Christ."
1 Corinthians 15:55-57

"The Lord has comforted his people, and will have mercy on his afflicted."
Isaiah 49:138 (AKJV)

"God will wipe away every tear from their eyes; there shall be no more death, nor sorrow, nor crying. There shall be no more pain, for the former things have passed away."
Revelation 21:4 (NKJV)

GUIDANCE

"The Lord himself goes before you and will be with you; he will
never leave you nor forsake you."
Deuteronomy 31:8 (NIV)

"Trust in the Lord with all your heart and lean not on your own
understanding; in all your ways acknowledge him, and he will
make your paths straight."
Proverbs 3:5-6 (NIV)

"Take delight in the Lord, and he will give you the desires of your
heart. Commit your way to the Lord; trust in him and he will do
this: He will make your righteous reward shine like the dawn, your
vindication like the noonday sun."
Psalm 37:4-6 (NIV)

GUILT

"The Lord is compassionate and gracious, slow to anger, abounding
in love. He will not always accuse, nor will he harbor his anger
forever; he does not treat us as our sins deserve or repay us
according to our iniquities. For as high as the heavens are above
the earth, so great is his love for those who fear him; as far as the
east is from the west, so far has he removed our transgressions
from us. As a father has compassion on his children, so the Lord
has compassion on those who fear him"
Psalm 103:8-13 (NIV)

"Come to me, all you who are weary and burdened,
and I will give you rest."
Matthew 11:28 (NIV)

HEALING

"Who Himself bore our sins in His own body on the tree, that we, having died to sins, might live for righteousness—
by whose stripes you were healed."
1 Peter 2:24 (NKJV)

"Heal me, O Lord, and I shall be healed; save me, and
I shall be saved, for you are my praise."
Jeremiah 17:14

"Therefore strengthen the hands which hang down, and the feeble knees, and make straight paths for your feet, so that what is lame may not be dislocated, but rather be healed. Pursue peace with all people, and holiness, without which no one will see the Lord."
Hebrews 12:11-14 (NKJV)

HEALTH

"'I will restore health to you And heal you of your wounds,'
says the Lord."
Jeremiah 30:17 (NKJV)

"Pleasant words are like a honeycomb, sweetness to soul
and health to the bones."
1 Corinthians 9:27

HEARING GOD'S VOICE

"Obey my voice, and I will be your God, and ye shall be my people: and walk ye in all the ways that I have commanded you,
that it may be well unto you."
Jeremiah 7:23 (NKJV)

"When he brings out his own sheep, he goes before them; and
the sheep follow him, for they know his voice. Yet they will by no
means follow a stranger, but will flee from him, for they do not
know the voice of strangers."
John 10:4-5 (NKJV)

"Now it shall come to pass, if you diligently obey the voice of the
Lord your God, to observe carefully all His commandments which
I command you today, that the Lord your God will set you high
above all nations of the earth."
Deuteronomy 28:1 (NKJV)

"He is our God, and we are his people of his pasture, and the sheep
of his hand. Today, if you will hear his voice,
harden not your hearts."
Psalm 95:7-8

HONESTY

"The Lord delights in men who are truthful."
Proverbs 12:22

"The Lord says: 'These people come near to me with their mouth
and honor me with their lips, but their hearts are far from me.'"
Isaiah 29:13 (NIV)

Don't be moved or swayed by the way things appear. Stand up
for the truth, all the time and everywhere you go! That is real
integrity, being complete or whole. It means being all that you are
and wherever you are. Acting one way here and another way there
shows hypocrisy, not integrity.
*** A shared thought on honesty ***

HOPE

"I am the Lord; those who hope in me will not be disappointed."
Isaiah 49:23 (NIV)

"You have been my hope, O Sovereign Lord,
my confidence since my youth."
Psalm 71:5 (NIV)

"Why are you downcast, O my soul? Why so disturbed within me?
Put your hope in God, for I will yet praise him,
my Savior and my God".
Psalm 42:11 (NIV)

HUMLITY

"With humility comes wisdom."
Proverbs 11:2

"All of you, clothe yourselves with humility toward one another,
because, 'God opposes the proud but shows favor to the humble.'
Humble yourselves, therefore, under God's mighty hand, that he
may lift you up in due time."
1 Peter 5:5-6 (NIV)

JOY

"This is the day the Lord has made; let us rejoice and be glad in it."
Psalm 118:24 (NIV)

"Though you have not seen him, you love him; and even though
you do not see him now, you believe in him and are filled with an
inexpressible and glorious joy, for you are receiving the end result
of your faith, the salvation of your souls."
1 Peter 1:8-9 (NIV)

"The fruit of the Spirit is love, joy, peace, longsuffering, gentleness,
goodness, faith, Meekness, temperance: against such
there is no law."
Galatians 5:22-23

"Shout aloud and sing for joy, for great is the Holy One of Israel."
Isaiah 12:6

"May the righteous be glad and rejoice before God; may they be
happy and joyful. Sing to God, sing in praise of his name, extol
him who rides on the clouds rejoice before him—
his name is the Lord."
Psalm 68:3-4

KEEPING PROMISES

"It better not to vow than to make a vow and not fulfill it."
Ecclesiastes 5:5 (NIV)

"Moses said to the heads of the tribes of Israel: 'This is what the
Lord commands: [2] When a man makes a vow to the Lord or takes
an oath to obligate himself by a pledge, he must not break his word
but must do everything he said.'"
Numbers 30:1-2 (NIV)

"If you make a vow to the Lord your God, do not be slow to pay it,
for the Lord your God will certainly demand it of you and you will
be guilty of sin. But if you refrain from making a vow, you will not
be guilty. Whatever your lips utter you must be sure to do, because
you made your vow freely to the Lord your God
with your own mouth."
Deuteronomy 23:21-23 (NIV)

LOVE

"Now this how we know what love is: Jesus Christ laid down his life for us. And we ought to lay down our lives for our brothers. If anyone of us has material possessions, and sees his brother in need but has no pity on him? Dear children, let us not love with words or tongue but with actions and in truth."
1 John 3:16-18

"If anyone says, 'I love God,' yet hates his brother, he is a liar. For anyone who does not love his brother, whom he has seen, cannot love God, whom he has not seen. And he has given us this command: Whoever loves God must also love his brother."
1 John 4:20-21 (NIV)

"Love is patient, love is kind. It does not envy, it does not boast, it is not proud. It is not rude, it is not self-seeking, it is not easily angered, it keeps no record of wrongs. Love does not delight in evil but rejoices with the truth. It always protects, always trusts, always hopes, always perseveres. Love never fails."
1 Corinthians 13: 4-8 (NIV)

"What does the Lord your God ask of you but to fear the Lord your God, to walk in all his ways, to love him, to serve the Lord your God with all your heart and with all your soul, and to observe the Lord's commands and decrees that I am giving you today for your own good?"
Deuteronomy 10:12-13 (NIV)

"He who has My commandments and keeps them, it is he who loves Me. And he who loves Me will be loved by My Father, and I will love him and manifest Myself to him."
John 14: 21 (NKJV)

"God so loved the world, that He gave His only begotten Son, that
whoever believes in Him shall not perish, but have eternal life."
John 3:16 (NASB)

MONEY

"A little that the righteous man hath is better than
the riches of many wicked."
Psalm 37: 16

"'Bring the whole tithe into the storehouse, that there may be food
in my house. Test me in this,' says the Lord Almighty, 'and see if I
will not throw open the floodgates of heaven and pour out so much
blessing that you will not have room enough for it.'"
Malachi 3:10 (NIV)

OBEDIENCE

"Obedience is better than sacrifice."
1 Samuel 15:22 (NLT)

"Though he was a Son, yet he learned obedience by
the things which he suffered."
Hebrews 5:8 (Webster)

"We should obey God rather than men."
Acts 5:29

"Those things, which ye have both learned, and received, and
heard, and seen in me, do: and the God of peace shall be with you."
Philippians 4:9

PATIENCE

"For ye have need of patience, that, after ye have done the
will of God, ye might receive the promise."
Hebrews 10:36

"My brethren, count it all joy when ye fall into divers temptations;
Knowing this, that the trying of your faith worketh patience. But
let patience have her perfect work, that ye may be perfect and
entire, wanting nothing."
James 1:2-4

"And not only so, but we glory in tribulations also: knowing that
tribulation worketh patience; And patience, experience;
and experience, hope."
Romans 5:3-4

PEACE

"The God of peace will crush Satan under your feet shortly. The
grace of our Lord Jesus Christ be with you. Amen."
Romans 16: 20 (NKJV)

"Peace I leave with you, my peace I give to you: not as the world
gives, give I to you. Let not your heart be troubled,
neither let it be afraid."
John 14:27 (AKJV)

"Let the peace of God rule in your hearts, to which also you are
called in one body; and be thankful."
Colossians 3:15 (KJ2000)

"Do not be anxious about anything, but in everything, by prayer and petition, with thanksgiving, present your requests to God. And the peace of God, which transcends all understanding, will guard your hearts and your minds in Christ Jesus."
Philippians 4:6-7 (NIV)

"I have told you these things, so that in me you may have peace. In this world you will have trouble. But take heart!
I have overcome the world."
John 16:33 (NIV)

PERSEVERANCE

"Blessed is the man who perseveres under trial, because when he has stood the test, he will receive the crown of life that God has promised to those who love him."
James 1: 12 (NIV)

"Pursue righteousness, godliness, faith, love, endurance and gentleness. Fight the good fight of the faith."
1 Timothy 6:11-12 (NIV)

PRAISE AND WORSHIP

"Therefore by Him let us continually offer the sacrifice of praise to God, that is, the fruit of our lips, giving thanks to His name."
Hebrews 13:15 (NKJV)

"You are a chosen generation, a royal priesthood, a holy nation, a people for his own; that you should show forth the praises of him who has called you out of darkness into his marvelous light."
1 Peter 2:9 (KJ2000)

"Praise the Lord! For it is good to sing praises to our God;
for it is pleasant, and praise beautiful."
Psalm 147:1

"I will call upon the Lord, who is worthy to be praised:
so shall I be saved from mine enemies."
2 Samuel 22:4

"I will bless the Lord at all times; His praise shall
continually be in my mouth."
Psalm31:1

PRAYER

"And it shall come to pass, that before they call, I will answer;
and while they are yet speaking, I will hear."
Isaiah 65:24

"And whatsoever ye shall ask in my name, that will I do,
that the Father may be glorified in the Son."
John 14:13

"Ask, and it shall be given you; seek, and ye shall find; knock,
and it shall be opened unto you."
Matthew 7:7

"The Lord is near to all who call upon Him, To all who call upon
Him in truth. He will fulfill the desire of those who fear Him; He
will also hear their cry and will save them."
Psalm 145:18-19 (NASB)

"Call unto me, and I will answer you, and show you great and
mighty things, which you know not."
Jeremiah 33:3 (KJ2000)

"Be joyful always; pray continually; give thanks in all circumstances, for this is God's will for you in Christ Jesus."
1 Thessalonians 5:16-18

"Confess your faults one to another, and pray one for another, that ye may be healed. The effectual fervent prayer of a righteous man availeth much."
James 5:16

"And call upon me in the day of trouble: I will deliver thee, and thou shalt glorify me."
Psalm 50:15

PROSPERITY

"If the iron be blunt, and he do not whet the edge, then must he put to more strength: but wisdom is profitable to direct."
Ecclesiastes 10:10

"And you shall remember the Lord your God, for it is He who gives you power to get wealth, that He may establish His covenant which He swore to your fathers, as it is this day."
Deuteronomy 8:18 (NKJV)

"Beloved, I pray that you may prosper in all things and be in health, just as your soul prospers."
3 John 1:2

REPENTANCE

"Repent, and be baptized, everyone of you, in the name of Jesus Christ for the forgiveness of sins, and you will receive the gift of the Holy Spirit. For the promise is to you, and to your children,

and to all who are far off, even as many as the Lord our
God will call to himself."
Acts 2:38-39 (WEB)

RESTORATION

"The Lord raise those who are bowed down;
the Lord loves the righteous."
Psalm 146:8

"He restores my soul: he leads me in the paths of
righteousness for his name's sake."
Psalm 23:3 (KJ2000)

"I will restore to you the years that the swarming locust has eaten,
You shall eat in plenty and be satisfied, and praise the name of
the Lord your God, who has dealt wondrously with you; and My
people, shall never be put to shame."
Joel 2:25-26

SEEKING GOD'S FACE

"But seek ye first the kingdom of God, and his righteousness; all
these things shall be added unto you."
Matthew 7:5

"Seek ye the Lord while he may be found,
call ye upon him while he is near."
Isaiah 55:6

"And ye shall seek me, and find me, when ye shall
search for me with all your heart."
Jeremiah 29:13 (ASV)

"But without faith it is impossible to please him: for he that cometh
to God must believe that he is, and that he is a rewarder of them
that diligently seek him."
Hebrews 11:6

"The Lord is with you, while ye be with him; and if ye seek him, he
will be found of you; but if ye forsake him, he will forsake you."
2 Chronicle 15:2

"Sow to yourselves I righteousness, reap in mercy; break up your
hallow ground: for it is time to seek the Lord, till he come
and rain righteousness upon you."
Hosea 10:12

SELF-CONTROL

"I discipline my body and bring it into subjection, lest when I
preached to others, I myself should be disqualified."
1 Corinthians 9:27

"Casting down arguments and every high thing that exalts itself
against the knowledge of God, bringing every thought into
captivity to the obedience of Christ."
2 Corinthians 10:5 (NKJV)

"Let your heart therefore be loyal to the Lord our God, to walk in
His statues and keep His commandants, as this day."
1 Kings 8:60-61

"Be doers of word, and not hearers only, deceiving yourselves."
James 1:22

SELF-ESTEEM

"For we are his workmanship, created in Christ Jesus for good works, which God afore prepared that we should walk in them."
Ephesians 2:10 (ASV)

"You are a chosen generation, a royal priesthood, a holy nation, His own special people, that you may proclaim the praises of Him who called you out of darkness into His marvelous light."
1 Peter 2:9 (NKJV)

"The Lord takes pleasure in His people; He will beautify the humble with salvation."
Psalm 149:4

"Your hands have made me and fashioned me: give me understanding, that I may learn your commandments. They that fear you will be glad when they see me; because I have hoped in your word."
Psalm 119:73-74 (KJ2000)

"If *anyone* be in Christ, he is a *new creation*; *old things have passed away*; behold, *all things have become new.*"
2 Corinthians 5:17

"Being confident of this very thing, that he who has begun a good work in you will perform it until the day of Jesus Christ."
Philippians 1:6 (KJ2000)

SPIRTUAL GROWTH

"Train yourself to be godly. For physical training is of some value, but godliness has value for all things, holding promise for both the present life and the life to come."
1 Timothy 4: 7-8

"When I Paul, was a child, I talked like a child; I thought like a child, I reasoned like a child. When I became a man, I put away childish ways behind me."
1 Corinthians 13:11

"God's divine power has given us everything we need for life and goodness. Through these he has given us his goodness. Through these he has given us his very great and precious promises, so that through them you may participate in the divine nature and escape the corruption in the world caused by evil desires. For this very reason, make every effort to add to your faith goodness; and to goodness, knowledge; and to knowledge, self-control; and to self-control, perseverance; and to perseverance, godliness, and to godliness, brotherly kindness; and to brotherly kindness, love. For if you possess these qualities in increasing measure, they will keep you from being ineffective and unproductive in your knowledge of our Lord Jesus Christ."
2 Peter 1:3-8

STRESS

"Be still, and know that I am God."
Psalm 46:10 (ESV)

"Come near to God and he will come near to you."
James 4:8 (NIV)

"O' Lord, you are my God, I will exalt you and praise your name. You have been a refuge for the poor, a refuge for the needy in his distress, a shelter from the storm and a shade from the heat."
Isaiah 25:1-4

"The Lord is my shepherd, I shall not want. He makes me lie down in green pastures; He leads me beside quiet waters. He restores my soul; He guides me in the paths of righteousness For

His name's sake. Even though I walk through the valley of the shadow of death, I fear no evil, for You are with me; Your rod and Your staff, they comfort me. You prepare a table before me in the presence of my enemies; You have anointed my head with oil; My cup overflows. Surely goodness and lovingkindness will follow me all the days of my life, And I will dwell in the house of the Lord forever."
Psalm 23 (NASB)

"Trust in the Lord with all your heart And do not lean on your own understanding. In all your ways acknowledge Him, And He will make your paths straight."
Proverbs 3: 5-6 (NASB)

"Blessed be the God and Father of our Lord Jesus Christ, the Father of mercies and God of all comfort, who comforts us in all our affliction so that we will be able to comfort those who are in any affliction with the comfort with which we ourselves are comforted by God. For just as the sufferings of Christ are ours in abundance, so also our comfort is abundant through Christ. But if we are afflicted, it is for your comfort and salvation; or if we are comforted, it is for your comfort, which is effective in the patient enduring of the same sufferings which we also suffer; and our hope for you is firmly grounded, knowing that as you are sharers of our sufferings, so also you are sharers of our comfort."
2 Corinthians 1:3-7 (NASB)

"Consider it all joy, my brethren, when you encounter various trials, knowing that the testing of your faith produces endurances. And let endurance have it perfect result, so that you may be perfect and complete, lacking in nothing. But if any of you lacks wisdom, let him ask of God, who gives to all generously and without reproach, and it will be given to him."
James 1: 2-5

"Come to me, all who are weary and heavy-laden, and I will give
you rest. Take my yoke upon you and learn from me, for I am
gentle and humble in heart, *and you will find rest for your souls.* For
my yoke is easy and my burden is light."
Matthew 11:28-30

SUFFERING

"There was given me a thorn in my flesh, a messenger of Satan, to
torment me. Three times I pleaded with the Lord to take it away
from me. But he said to me, 'My grace is sufficient for you, for my
power is made perfect in weakness.' Therefore I will boast all the
more gladly about my weaknesses, so that Christ's power may rest
on me. That is why, for Christ's sake, I delight in weaknesses, in
insults, in hardships, in persecutions, in difficulties. For when I am
weak, then I am strong."
2 Corinthians 12: 7-10 (NIV)

"The God of all grace, who called you to his eternal glory in Christ,
after you have suffered a little while, will himself restore you and
make you strong, firm and steadfast."
1 Peter 5:10 (NIV)

"Those who suffer; God delivers in their suffering; he speaks to
them in their affliction."
Job 36: 15

"My comfort in my suffering in this: Your promise
preserves my life, O' Lord."
Psalm 119:50

"Consider it pure joy, my brothers, whenever you face trials of many kinds, because you know that the testing of your faith develops perseverance. Perseverance must finish its work so that you may be mature and complete, not lacking anything."
James 1: 2-4

TALENTS

"A man's gift makes room for him And brings him before great men."
Proverbs 18:16 (NASB)

"Commit your works to the Lord, And your thoughts will be established."
Proverbs 16:3 (NKJV)

"We have not received, not the spirit of the world, but the Spirit who is from God, that we might know the things that have been freely given to us by God."
1 Corinthians 2:12

"To who much is given, from him much will be required."
Luke 12:28
*** Let us pursue our God-given passion. ***

TEMPTATIONS

"No temptation has seized you except what is common to man. And God is faithful; he will not let you be tempted beyond what you can bear. But when you are tempted, he will also provide a way out so that you can stand up under it."
1 Corinthians 10:13 (NIV)

"When tempted, no one should say, 'God is tempting me.' For God cannot be tempted by evil, nor does he tempt anyone."
James 1:13 (NIV)

"Resist the devil and he will flee from you."
James 4:7 (NASB)

"Let us hold firmly to the faith we profess. For we do not have a high priest who is unable to sympathize with our weakness, but we have one who has been tempted in every way, just as we are, yet was without sin. Let us then approach the throne of grace with confidence, so that we may receive mercy and find grace to help us in our time of need."
Hebrews 4:14-16

Whenever temptations arise, in whatever situation, fall back on the written Word of God concerning it, just as our Lord Jesus Christ did when He was tempted by the Devil.
A word of encouragement

TRUST

"Trust in the Lord with all your heart and lean not on your own understanding; in all your ways acknowledge him, and he will make your paths straight."
Proverbs 3:5-6

"Trust in the Lord, and do good; so shalt thou dwell in the land, and verily thou shalt be fed. Delight thyself also in the Lord; and he will give thee the desires of thy heart. Commit thy way to the Lord; trust also in him; and he will bring it to pass."
Psalm 37:3-5 (Webster)

UNITY

"Now I plead with you, brethren, by the name of our Lord Jesus Christ, that you all speak the same thing, and that there be no divisions among you, but that you be perfectly joined together in the same mind and in the same judgment."
1 Corinthians 1:10 (NKJV)

"Can two walk together, unless they are agreed?"
Amos 3:3 (NKJV)

"Now may the God of patience and comfort grant you to be like-minded toward one another, according to Christ Jesus, that you may with one mind and one mouth glorify the God and Father of our Lord Jesus Christ. Therefore receive one another, just as Christ also received us, to the glory of God."
Romans 15:5-7 (NKJV)

A house divided cannot stand.

A word of thought

WISDOM

"If any man lacks wisdom, he should ask God, who gives generously to all without finding fault, and it will be given to him."
James 1:5

He who walks with wise grows wise, but a companion
of fools suffers harm.
Proverbs 13:20

"My son, if you accept my words and store up my commands
within you, turning your ear to wisdom and applying your heart
to understand, and if you call out for insight and cry out aloud for
understanding, and if you look for it as if silver and search for it as
for hidden treasure, then you will understand the fear of the Lord
and find the knowledge of God."
Proverbs 2:1-5

"Wisdom is supreme; therefore get wisdom. Though it cost all you
have, get understanding."
Proverbs 4:7 (NIV)

How does a person become wise? One must first begin to listen.
Wisdom is freely available to those who will stop talking and start
paying attention to God and His Word, to parents, and to wise
counselors.

Proverbs tells us that wisdom is not reserved for the brainy people
alone and that becoming wise requires self-discipline to study and
humbly seek wisdom at every opportunity.

Words to think on

Prophetic Words

Don't you know that I have the resources for this? I have not planned your life only to leave out what you need to accomplish my plans. I am more than this.

You have longed to see the provision, and I have longed for you to see me. When you are truly broken and your desire is for me alone, then you will be ready.

When you desire my face more than my hand, you shall know a joy in ministry that has always been elusive to you. My purpose shall stand.

You belong to me exclusively, and I will not be slack in my promise. I have already conquered, and I pass the rewards of victory along to my children.

JESUS

CONTACT INFORMATION

To contact Rev. Antonio Sherman for ministry or to purchase of any of his products, please write to

P.O. Box 3789
Columbia, SC 29230

You can also write to us if the Lord has laid it on your heart to be a blessing to this ministry in any way. We want you to know that whatever you give is prayed over and used solely for the furthering of the work of the ministry. "Our goal is to have as many of these books printed or ordered as possible, and we want to send them out worldwide to get as many copies as possible into the hands of the unsaved and of those who don't truly understand salvation according to the written Word of God, here and in the uttermost parts of the world, as commissioned by our Lord and Savior Jesus Christ."

Rev. Antonio Sherman is bishop/overseer of the following outreach ministries: True Light Holiness Temple in Jesus Christ
Ministries of Help & Encouragement
Suffer Not the Children Foundation
Urban Inspirational Music Ministry
True Word Records Music Ministry
True Light Praise Dance & Drama Ministry
Seeing the Light Bible Study Ministry,
which can be seen broadcast live every on ustream.tv and where everyone is welcome to come sit in and be a part of the group as we pray, study, and believe the Word of God.

About the Author

Antonio Sherman is an individual who personally has seen and experienced the miracle-working hand of God in his personal life and that of those who surround him at home and abroad. He has seen God's saving grace and divine intervention in many forms. He is a true believer whom God has revealed himself to in his earlier walk with Him. But he is also a father, a husband, and a full-time student at Columbia International University. One of their mottoes is "Get to know Him . . . to make Him known." Antonio is studying for a double major in Pastoral Ministries and Bible Major.

He has served the Lord as associate pastor, pastor, minister, Sunday school teacher, elder, and bishop, but truly as an undeserving, but blessed, child of God, because of Jesus Christ. Antonio sees himself only as servant of the One and Only True Living God—I AM.

This book, *Salvation: A Gift from God*, is a partial autobiography that shares some personal testimonies and experiences. But this book is all true and all reality, and the whole truth of how salvation can be yours and has been given to all as a gift.

Because the Lord has led you to be holding a copy of this book, please read it and accept God's gift. His gift has already been paid for by *Jesus*!

"By grace you have been saved through faith, and that not of yourselves; it *is the gift of God*, not of works, lest anyone should boast."
Ephesians 2:8-9

An Afterword from the Author

A Word of Acknowledgment and Prayer

I would like to give the highest praise and honor to God my Father; to Jesus Christ, my personal Lord and Savior; and to the Holy Spirit, who is in charge. I thank God for choosing me to be deemed worthy enough to be the vessel charged to go tell His people to believe in His promises and in His Word and to walk in them.

I would also like to thank my lovely wife, Shamika, whom I love dearly, for being patient as the Lord dealt with me in putting this book together, for the time it took from her, as me being a husband. I thank God for blessing us with a beautiful son, Judah Zion, who binds the ties of our family together as a whole.

I pray that God adds a blessing to the readers of this book who read it with a sincere heart, seeking to understand; seeking how to receive salvation, the gift from God; and desiring to walk in the promises of God that have been given to us all though Jesus Christ.

In knowing that the Word of God is true and that He is a man who can not lie but who is able to bring every promise to pass that He has given within His Holy Scripture, it is in the precious and mighty name of Jesus Christ that I pray, giving God the glory forever and ever.

Amen.